Robin Specular

BRICKS
TO
BRIDGES

Make Your Strategy Come Alive

BRIDGES™
BUSINESS CONSULTANCY INT.

www.bridgesconsultancy.com

TESTIMONIALS

"In his book, Robin Speculand provides with clarity, simplicity, focus on relevance and creativity a powerful and practical tool for managers and executives who want to succeed in one of the most critical challenges in the current business environment–strategy implementation. A must read..."

Elcio Paulo Pereira
Latin America Training & Development Center Director
Citigroup International

"After working with Robin over the last year we have been able to adopt first-hand many of the excellent practical tips and hands-on ideas in this book that has allowed the bank to not only implement our strategy but also ensure delivery on performance. It is a book fellow leaders should read just to find the one gem that can transform their company and along the way pick up so much more."

Andrew C. Stevens
CEO
Commercial bank
State of Qatar

"Full of good practical insight and advice on strategy implementation, this book explains how planning strategy is only the first stage and implementation remains a key differentiator in business today. Based on solid research, it clearly explains what it means and how to bring the critical elements of implementation together, while offering sound practical advice about how to make things happen."

David Shackleton
Senior Vice President & Area Managing Director
Australia, New Zealand & Fiji
Starwood Hotels & Resorts

"True to its promise, this book takes the headache and heartache out of figuring out one of toughest challenges in corporate reality–bridging the strategy and implementation divide. Quick, grab that Implementation Compass and start to make things happen in your market space."

Dr. Prem N. Shamdasani
Director of APEX MBA Program
National University of Singapore Business School

"Leaders appreciate short, sharp, easy-to-use tips and techniques that explain what works and what does not. The ideas in this book are easy to use, impactful and visually pleasing: a very powerful prompter."

Jill Dodwell-Groves
Head of Executive Development
Jardine Matheson

"If I get one actionable idea from a book, it's more than paid for itself. Robin's book is packed with an abundance of actionable ideas that I am adopting into my own organization and on behalf of our clients. It is a page turner that you just do not want to put down as you pick up one great idea after the other. Start reading it today and you will be transformed in the way you view strategy and its implementation."

Bruce Scheer
Founder and Partner
FutureSight Consulting LLC, USA

"Bricks to Bridges is what you need to read if you want to make things happen rather than wonder why your strategy never took off. It is a practical engaging guide which leads you along the path of successful implementation. While based on a solid conceptual framework, it is also full of action items with lots of concrete case studies to illustrate how these might be applied."

Lori Figueiredo
Learning Strategist

"A very easy and fun-to-read book. It is a pure genius piece of work to deliver such a heavy subject of strategy implementation in such an inspirational way. The advice offered is equally right to the point and practical. Knowing Robin personally, this can only be his signature."

Hans Peter Brenner
President Asia Pacific
B Braun Medical Industries

"We have long known that executing strategy is far harder than creating it. My own work in the area of organisational alignment and customer experience management has convinced me that without a systematic method of implementation, strategic planning can become a hollow exercise. This highly readable book gives practical tips for implementing strategy and guides you on how to make it come alive in your organization."

Shaun Smith
Author of *"Managing the Customer Experience–turning customers into advocates"*
and *"Uncommon practice-people who deliver a great brand experience"*

"This is an essential read that should be made universally available. Enjoy, refer and recommend this bridge to progress for yourself and your colleagues."

From an unbiased Father in Scotland

Bridges Business Consultancy Int.
5 Shenton Way, #37-02 UIC Building
Singapore 068808

First edition July 2005
Published by Bridges Business Consultancy Int.

Cover design, illustrations, typography and
page layout by Litt Lindden Design Associates
(Tel:+65 6294 9868, Website: http://www.littlindden.com)

Printed in Great Britain by TJ International Ltd, Padstow, Cornwall.

FOR ORDERING INFORMATION, CONTACT:
Bridges Business Consultancy Int.
5 Shenton Way, #37-02 UIC Building
Singapore 068808
Republic of Singapore
E-mail: bridges@bridgesconsultancy.com
Website: www.bridgesconsultancy.com

"Only a successful implementation will power a strategy forward."

CONTENTS

*"To my parents who continue
to be a guiding light."*

Forward for Bricks to Bridges
by Ron Kaufman

Since 1985, I have worked with hundreds of organizations on thousands of good ideas, great dreams and bold visions. In almost every case, the people involved are talented, focused and sincere. They are motivated by achieving what's possible for their organizations and themselves.

But these same people can also become cautious with their ideas, cynical about their dreams, even resentful and resigned about their visions.

How can this happen? What explains this obvious contradiction?

Robin Speculand has spent years wrestling with this problem, unraveling this difficult dilemma. He has now discovered its cause and has found the keys and tools to resolve it.

Here's what Robin discovered:

Creating strategy is an uplifting thing to do. It clarifies who you are, what you want, where you want to go and more importantly, how you are going to get there. Creating strategy is energizing and motivating. It gives you a sense of purpose and direction. It makes you feel alive.

Creating strategy is also heady stuff. Think vision, mission and values. Think management retreats, board meetings, research studies, PEST and SWOT analyses and scenario planning. The tools and techniques for creating strategy are well defined. All of these lead to choices, decisions and ambition.

But Robin also discovered something else:

Implementing strategy is hard. It's messy and it's unpredictable. The toolset is fragmented, inconsistent and often incomplete. Implementing strategy can be a difficult exercise in answering questions, changing behaviors and overcoming resistance. It is fraught with contradictions, setbacks and throwbacks. It is diverse and simultaneous and uncertain.

Let me give you some examples.

My specialty is helping organizations achieve superior service, increase customer loyalty, build strong partnerships and create dynamic teams. Everyone can get behind these ideas. They make for great visions, wonderful objectives and strategic intentions stated in these ways: Delightful Customer Experience, Putting the Customer First, Total Customer Focus, Absolute Customer Obsession, We Are Customer Driven, Delivering Customer Delight, World-Class Customer Service, 100% Customer Retention, Outstanding Customer Loyalty and, of course, The Customer is King.

But in these same organizations, I have seen the following realities arise:

Senior managers announce a new strategy, middle managers struggle to understand it and frontline staff ignore it from the beginning as "just another initiative" that goes nowhere.

Marketing sends out transcripts and videos of the big boss making a new strategic statement but nothing changes in the way work gets done day to day.

New policies are launched and expensive software is installed but little training is provided to help staff get through the transition.

Customers are promised higher service standards but the internal criteria for staff appraisal, pay and promotion are financial only and remain unchanged.

These inconsistencies are just the tip of the iceberg. If you've been in business for more than a few years, you can add painful and expensive examples of your own.

In a world of high-speed, interconnected, always—on communications, how can organizations be so incoherent and incompetent when it comes to implementing their strategies on the ground?

After studying this book *Bricks to Bridges*, you will see how clear the answers become.

Implementing new strategy often requires a fundamental change in thinking, standards, practices, procedures, expectations, communications and more. And until now, no one has offered a comprehensive guide to integrating these changes so they work synergistically, even exponentially. Until now, no one has shown you how to successfully and comprehensively implement your strategy, regardless of what strategy you choose and which industry or competitive situation you may be in.

Sure, great leaders in business, sports and government have offered their advice in best-selling books and speeches. But what they know derives from their decisions made during their influential times. These decisions simply may not work in yours. It's like going camping and someone teaches you how to buy and pitch a tent but you find out too late that you also needed to bring waterproof boots.

You really need someone who can show you the whole picture all at once and help you see how the pieces are connected—someone who can show you which tools to use, teach you how to use them and then hand over the entire toolkit in a smoothly working set.

You need someone who has worked with scores of organizations in many industries on multiple strategies in countless situations. And you need someone who takes the time to capture all that understanding and put it in a form you can use and even enjoy.

In fact, what you need is exactly what you hold in your hands, right here and right now. Robin Speculand has done the work required. And *Bricks to Bridges* contains all the answers that you seek.

Robin sees strategy implementation for what it really is: a four-dimensional maze filled with blind alleys, hard turns and dead ends. Many organizations dive into the maze with great fanfare and excitement ("Our new strategy is launched!") but almost as many give up or give in, drifting along lost inside.

To get through the maze, you need a map, a compass and a guide to show you the way. *Bricks to Bridges* gives you all three.

Want proof? Simply start by looking through this book.

One of the great challenges facing authors today is engaging readers enough so they will actually study the entire book. Robin has created unique ways to capture your attention and keep you interested, page after unusual page. And he's made it easy for you to go back at any time to check the highlights and review them.

Go ahead, take a look. Just start flipping the pages and you will notice how well Robin has deployed this strategy. You will see that the book's unique response to challenge, its extraordinary effort and its unrelenting desire to find a better way characterizes the man who wrote it.

I first met Robin in the early 1990s in Macau. I told him, "If you ever want a job in Singapore, let me know." And later that day, he did.

We brought him to the Service Quality Centre where he soon became the Manager of Business Development and set a pace for growth and excellence in service that remains the benchmark for achievement today.

He went on to Citibank and became a Regional Vice President for Service and Quality, learning an enormous amount all over the world and working to implement the company's global strategy in Asia Pacific.

Finally, Robin stepped out to launch Bridges Business Consultancy Int. and stepped in to the best work he's done yet, by far. This book is a culmination of where he's been, what he's learned and how he's passionate about sharing it all with you.

But if I know Robin, he's far from finished. And may never be. He's insatiable, persistent, always seeking, questioning, wondering if there's a better way.

If you take the advice he offers in this book, you will learn a lot for yourself as you help your organization succeed. But if you take my advice and keep this book as a treasure, you will gain even more. Rest assured, within a few years, Robin will write another one and teach us a lot more.

Wishing you the best in all your work—and in all your life—by applying the strategies Robin brings you in *Bricks to Bridges*.

Ron Kaufman
Author, Up Your Service! Singapore, 2005

Foreword to Bricks to Bridges
by Shaun Smith

In my work with organisations around the world, I am struck again and again by the sheer capacity for them to initiate well-intended programmes, projects and processes that fail to deliver value to themselves or their customers.

As an example, expenditure on Customer Relationship Management systems worldwide was calculated to total $46 billion dollars in 2004. Yet the research firm Gartner estimated that 55 percent of these systems actually dilute earnings and drive customers away—the very opposite of what was intended.

What is the problem? All too often, it is a failure of execution, an inability to align all parts of an organisation with a strategy's desired direction.

A few years ago, I designed my Organizational Alignment Survey™ to help executives identify alignment gaps in their organizations and bring people, processes and internal systems together into a harmonious whole—ready to deliver corporate strategy. This survey has successfully been used by leading companies around the world to improve their results, but it doesn't go far enough. Knowing where gaps are is a necessary—but insufficient—step towards closing them.

This is where *Bricks to Bridges* comes in.

In a world of theories, "gurus" and management models, it is refreshing to find a book packed with common-sense ideas and down-to-earth advice. Robin has forged his approach in the crucible of projects to help organisations move from strategy to reality. Although the concepts he addresses are common sense, they are still *uncommon* practice.

If you are responsible for helping implement strategy, then this book is for you. *Bricks to Bridges* is organised around the notion of the Implementation Compass. For strategic change to be adopted and then stick, each of the cardinal points represented on the Compass must be addressed. Points on the Compass include People, Communications, Culture and more. Case studies featured throughout illustrate how organisations can most effectively deal with these factors.

The need to create clear strategic direction and then manage organisational change to achieve it is a continuing process—or at least it should be. To this end, the stories, examples and tips in *Bricks to Bridges* will provide food for thought for some time to come. I encourage you to dip in to this book and *use* it, not simply read it. Once you become familiar with the insights it offers, you will find it occupying the most easily accessible spot on your bookshelf.

You have bought this book, presumably because you perceive that it can add value. Your intentions are sound; you have the means; you are now ready. Simply follow the advice of Nike and "Just do it." Open the book. Read a page. You won't regret it.

Shaun Smith is co-author of *Uncommon Practice—People who deliver a great brand experience*, and *Managing the Customer Experience—turning customers into advocates*.

Acknowledgments

Confucius is quoted as saying, "Find a job you love and you will never work another day in your life." I have been lucky enough to find my life's passion—making strategies come alive in organizations. In writing this book, I aim to share with you the tools, techniques and experience I have gained that will enable you to successfully and profitably implement your strategy.

Writing *Bricks to Bridges* has been a pleasure and I hope you will enjoy reading it as much as I did writing it. Over the 24 months in taking this book from concept to reality, colleagues and friends have given me indubitable support. Ron Kaufman is not only a friend and mentor but also an inspiration and motivation. Thank you, Ron, for taking the time in your ever-demanding schedule to write the foreword to *Bricks to Bridges*.

Litt Lindden Design Associates (Singapore) accepted the daunting task of turning a raw manuscript into a visual work of art. Creative Director Suvajit Das and his team, especially Art Director Lysandra Lewis, have done an amazing job and have earned my enduring thanks.

The content of the book has gone through many refinements to bring it to its current high level of quality. For taking time to add tremendous value to the initial manuscript, I would like to thank Michel Sznajer for his expertise in content feedback, editor Barbara McNichol for constantly improving the wording and coping with my misspelling, Duncan McMurdo and Venkat Narayanan for suggesting excellent improvements, Claire Astle for her continual support, encouragement and feedback and Dilip Mukerjea for his innovative inputs and guidance on how the brain works. I especially thank Walter S. Speculand for patiently reading and rereading the manuscript.

Introduction

Living high in the mountain, an old guru is renowned throughout the valley for his wisdom. One day, two young men decide to put the guru to a test. They catch a small bird in the forest at the foot of the mountain, then begin to climb it. They agree on the way they will hide the small bird behind their backs, then ask the guru whether it is dead or alive. If he says the bird is dead, they will open their hands and let the bird fly away. If he says the bird is alive, they will squeeze it in their hands to kill it. Either way, the guru will be proved wrong.

After days of trekking, they finally arrive at the top of the mountain. Standing before the guru, they ask, "Do you know what we have behind our backs?" The guru looks at the ground, strokes his long white beard and says, "A small bird." They then ask, "Is the bird dead or alive?" Again the guru looks at the ground. After several minutes, he slowly raises his head and replies, "Whether the bird lives or dies is up to you."

At the end of the day, whether or not your strategy implementation comes alive or dies is up to you.

Indeed, it's up to every individual in the organization to say "I am responsible" and follow that by taking the right action.

But where do you begin when you want to make your strategy come alive? And once you start, what comes next? It's tough enough just creating strategy, never mind implementing it.

Leaders in organizations devote tremendous amount of time identifying strategies that will outplay the competition, win market share and increase profits and shareholder value. But that is where the similarities end, for the strategies adopted can vary from improving customer service to moving operations overseas to China; from adopting a quality program to restructuring the entire organization.

When a strategy is implemented successfully and the right results are achieved, the cobweb-like difficulties encountered along the way become distant memories. Every successful implementation fosters an environment that's a pleasure to be part of: Business indicators are positive, market share grows, customers and staff are satisfied and the end of the financial year brings the promise of bonuses.

But when the strategy isn't successfully implemented, the opposite happens, right? Wrong!

In many organizations when a strategy fails to deliver the right results, the leaders either quickly amend it or they lower expectations to give the illusion it is working or they quickly adopt a new strategy to cover up the failure.

How often do you hear leaders declare "Our strategy failed"? They keep up a façade until a new and successful strategy kicks in. Then they quietly bury the old, failed strategy in the graveyard of, yep, failed strategies.

So just how do you go about making your organization's strategy come alive?

By first giving it a personality and character so that everyone concerned can relate to it and start to understand it. Then building it brick by brick until a bridge has been successfully constructed to reach the new frontier. At this point, the strategy has become part of the organization's DNA. Its leaders will know this has been achieved when the strategy is no longer a separate focus but becomes business as usual.

When you set out to adopt this book's guiding principles, *Bricks to Bridges* works as a compass to guide you through the hazardous implementation journey—which I call the implementation maze. The guiding principles impose a structure designed to make every implementation come alive. They highlight critical areas on your journey while spelling out what works and what doesn't. Most important, **they presents today's new thinking on strategy implementation**.

Lay of the Land for
Bricks to Bridges

Chapter 1 introduces many of the common challenges organizations come across when they move from creating strategy to implementing it.

Chapter 2 discusses the eight traditional and six new fundamentals of implementation. The eight traditional fundamentals focus on lessons learned from past implementations while the six new fundamentals are based on research conducted by Bridges Business Consultancy Int. (the organization where I work) over a five year period and the clients we work with which includes Citigroup, Singapore Airlines, Microsoft, Temasek Holdings, IBM, Government Investment Corporation of Singapore, AXA, VISA International, Maersk Sealand, Deutche Bank, Fullerton Hotel, Singapore Ministry of Defence, Singapore Power Group, Philips, OCBC Bank, Ikea, Reuters, Land Transport Authority of Singapore, Jardine Matheson, B Braun, Visa International, Maersk Sealand and Western Union. This chapter highlights further steps leaders can take toward strategy implementation.

Chapter 3 unravels the challenges ahead, going to the heart of what needs to happen to make your organization's strategy come alive.

Chapters 4 through to 13 guide you through a framework you can adopt and adapt to implement your strategy.

Chapter 14, the last chapter, looks at successful and failed actions in business in a fun way.

Callouts: You'll come across two types of callouts to assist you.
Watch Out! draws attention to the pitfalls and blind alleys that can cause strategies to fail.
This Works! features secret tips and shortcuts that will assist you on your way to successful implementation.

For quick recall, you'll find a complete list of the **Watch Out!** pitfalls and the **This Works!** tips at the end of each chapter. For a free soft copy of the **Watch Out!** and the **This Works!** list, send an email to bridges@bridgesconsultancy.com with "soft copy of **This Works!**" in the title.

Okay, so let's get your strategy implementation started!
Robin Speculand
June 2005

WATCH OUT!

Leaders spend too much time creating strategies and initiatives that fail to deliver the desired results because of poor implementation.

chapter 1
Houston,
we have a
Problem...

Let's start with the facts.

The corporate graveyard of strategy implementation is littered with organizations that have failed to make their strategies come alive. Despite the good intentions of the leaders,

9 out of 10 strategies
fail to deliver the desired results.[1]

Just think for a moment what this means: you have little or nothing to show for the time and investments you have spent creating the strategy, attending meetings, participating in conference calls, designing presentations, engaging external advice and preparing the organization.

Strategies are created to win market share, improve operations and service, beat the competition, launch new products and leverage technology to name just a few. But no matter the strategy and its objective more often than not it fails to deliver the results.

In their outstanding book *The Balanced Scorecard*[2], David Norton and Robert Kaplan noted that 90 percent of organizations fail to execute their strategies successfully.

A. Blanton Godfrey, Chairman and CEO of the Juran Institute, a Connecticut-based consultancy, claims that as few as 10 percent of technology initiatives deliver their anticipated benefits.

Douglas K. Smith, author of the book *Taking Charge of Change, 10 Principles for Managing People and Performance*[3] states that, "Even with significant financial and intellectual resources devoted to change, up to 80 percent on fundamental change efforts fail and companies revert to business as usual".

A long term study by Newcastle University, UK (1973-1989), showed that business success is governed more by how well strategies are implemented than how good the strategy is to begin with.

Bridges Business Consultancy Int. (hencefore called Bridges) surveyed businesses across Southeast Asia over a five year period and found that 90 percent of strategy implementations failed to deliver desired results.

Three Critical Implementation Questions

1. Why does Strategy Implementation have such a high failure rate?

2. Why do organizations keep repeating the same mistakes?

3. Why do managers tolerate a 90 percent failure rate?

Why does Strategy Implementation have such a High Failure Rate?

Before you even start to implement your strategy, as you have seen, the odds are stacked against you. To change the way people work and think—is not easy; to change the way they service and approach customers is not easy and to improve the internal work process is not easy.

Every day, thousands of organizations around the world are embarking on implementing their strategy, yet only a few make them work successfully. Billions of dollars are spent, millions of ideas are lost and a hundred thousand hours are wasted, because of unsuccessful implementation. Success happens when actual results match the desired results as they were spelled out at the beginning of the implementation.

After leaders have created the strategy, they frequently place too heavy an emphasis on the start of the strategy implementation and over time the momentum, passion and commitment wavers. At the start of the implementation, there is excitement around its launch and the sharing with the rest of the organization.

After a while, however, the daily operational issues or a crisis may distract them. Or they may simply lose enthusiasm as they move from the excitement of creating strategy to the ardous challenge of implementing it. Implementing strategy often takes considerable time and effort and requires tremendous focus and attention to detail.

Why do Organizations keep Repeating the Same Mistakes?

I have asked many different groups across the world why strategy implementation fails. Without much prompting, I always receive an avalanche of explanations. People know why strategy implementation fails in their organizations!

Why, therefore, do implementations keep failing, even when leaders know the reasons? If organizations know what goes wrong, why do they keep repeating the same mistakes?

Over the 40 years since strategy implementation first became a topic in business, leaders have failed to make any dramatic improvements in the way they approach implementation.

Different strategies emerge but their implementation is usually so poorly managed, the desired results rarely materialize.

If people know what goes wrong, why do they keep repeating the same mistakes?

Over the 40 years since strategy implementation first became a topic in business, leaders have failed to make any dramatic improvements in the way they approach implementation. Employees frequently implement new initiatives without even reviewing previous initiatives. Worse, they review the lessons learned from previous initiatives but fail to recognize and apply them because it takes an extra effort to speak to those responsible and ask their opinions. In some cases, there are cultural barriers to overcome. In addition, the task of reviewing documents about the implementation process can be laborious and time consuming.

Over the 40 years since strategy implementation first became a topic in business, leaders have failed to make any dramatic improvements to how they approach implementation.

Some organizations charge along on the road to failure, neither learning nor understanding why previous initiatives didn't work. Instead, they blindly repeat the same mistakes ending with the same failures—for the same reasons.

Why do
Leaders Tolerate
a 90 Percent Failure Rate?

Leaders tolerate a high failure rate because, until now, they have had no better methodology for implementing strategy. It's like asking why people tolerated a three-month boat trip to travel to Europe from the Far East 100 years ago, or why we used to buy vinyl records that scratched and ruined our favorite songs. 100 years ago, the steamship was the fastest way to travel between continents and just a few decades ago, music lovers only had a choice of vinyl records or cassette tapes.

The evolution of strategy implementation requires learning from past experiences. Just as movies have evolved from videos to laser discs to VCDs to DVDs, ways of implementing strategy are also evolving.

Over the years, leaders have become conditioned to expect strategy implementations

to fail. The profits of doom say, "I told you so" while some leaders simply ask "What's next?" The better question to ask is "What must we do differently next time?"

It is also important to ask why such a high failure rate is tolerated in this area but not in any other area of business—we would not accept a 90 percent failure rate for closing deals, a 90 percent rate of dissatisfied customers, or a 90 percent employee turnover rate. One major factor is that to date, leaders have focused more on *creating* strategy. Strategy creation is tough to get right and is still a relatively new topic in the development of business thinking. It's time, however, to put the spotlight on this failure rate to determine what it really takes to bring the strategy alive.

To do this, let's take a broad look at organizational transformation: the *one, two, three* of transformation.

One, Two, Three
of Transformation

Figure 1.1 shows a broad view of the three steps involved in transformation:

1. The vision, mission and values
2. Strategic creation
3. Strategy implementation

Step One: Vision, mission and values—sets the direction and purpose.

Step Two: Strategic creation—leads to the design of the strategy and tells us what we need to do.

Step Three: Strategy implementation—tells us how and what to focus on.

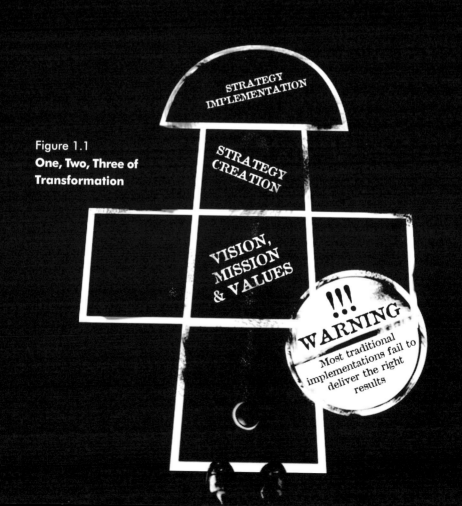

Figure 1.1
One, Two, Three of Transformation

STRATEGY IMPLEMENTATION

STRATEGY CREATION

VISION, MISSION & VALUES

!!! WARNING
Most traditional implementations fail to deliver the right results

Strategy Implementation
as We Know it Today

Strategy implementation typically encompasses everything that needs to happen after the creation of the strategy—specifically the communications, measurement, process redesign, changes to rewards and recognition programs and even the leadership, to name just a few!

Herein lies the first problem. Strategy implementation often ends up consisting of only a few of these activities or none at all. In fact, strategy implementation can simply consist of a town hall meeting in which the CEO shares the broad outline of the strategy and explains why the staff should adopt it.

Today, strategy implementation typically involves eight action areas that we can call the eight traditional fundamentals, to be detailed in Chapter Two:

- Communicating The Vision
- Identifying Obstacles
- Creating a Sense of Urgency
- Training
- Identifying Change Agents
- Altering Rewards & Recognition Process
- Setting & Celebrating Milestones
- Monitoring Progress

Successful implementation builds on these eight traditional fundamentals of strategy implementation—and more. It avoids the pitfalls that constantly get repeated, such as a lack of top management support, failing to develop a comprehensive plan of action, not creating a compelling case for change, not experiencing enough early successes, failing to change reward and recognition, delivering inconsistent and ineffective communication, missing the link between the change and the individual, overlooking those expected to implement the change and delegating responsibility without providing follow-through.

But hang on! We know all this. We've read the same message all over the place. What really works? What do we need to do to break the mold of previous failures and successfully implement our strategy?

INTRODUCING the
Implementation Compass

It allows you to:

1. Fully understand what it takes to implement your strategy

2. Assess your current strengths and weaknesses

3. Be guided through the implementation maze

4. Adopt best practices

5. Ensure longevity of your implementation

The Implementation Compass is a generic tool for guiding you through today's implementation challenges and embedding your strategy. It is a Bridges tool designed to make your strategy come alive.

Implementation Compass Guidelines

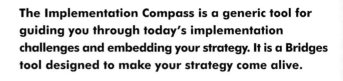

PEOPLE

REVIEW   BIZ CASE

REINFORCEMENT —— COMMUNICATION

PROCESS   MEASUREMENT

CULTURE

IMPLEMENTATION COMPASS

1. The Implementation Compass works for both small and large organizations.

2. Trying to implement strategy without a compass to guide you simply makes a difficult job more difficult!

3. Every organization's implementation is different and therefore each journey is unique.

4. Everyone starts from a different reference point.

5. You can still partly copy from other organizational implementation successes.

6. Each of the eight components is critically important and the degree of each one's importance varies within each organization. For example, one organization may need to spend more time on measurement while another should focus more on communication.

7. During the implementation, be ready for the energy level in the organization to dissipate—sometimes at an alarming rate—to the point of forcing the whole process to grind to a halt.

8. It's easy to get lost, distracted or turn down the wrong path along the way. Therefore, it's important to review constantly: where is the organization now, what has worked, what has not worked and are we heading in the right direction?

The Implementation Compass provides the framework for this book. Each chapter addresses in detail how you can use it as a tool to make your strategy come alive. But first, let's look at The Curse of Dissipating Energy.

The Curse of Dissipating Energy

When the Ancient Egyptians ruled, it was a great honor for kings or pharaohs to be buried in a pyramid with gold, jewels and other valuables. The Egyptian people believed death was just the beginning of a journey to the other world and that each individual's eternal life depended on the continued existence of the king. This belief made the safety of the pharaoh's tomb of great concern to the entire kingdom.

To protect the wealth that lay within the pyramid, the Egyptians built a great labyrinth to confuse any robber who dared enter the pyramid after it had been sealed. Not only was the labyrinth confusing, every step through it was likely to be filled with hidden trickery and booby traps. One never knew if the next step meant jumping over an unseen void, falling to the ground to avoid a blaze of fire, or dodging a blade that was so sharp it could dissect an invader in one swift motion. Not surprisingly, most robbers, initially filled with bravado, failed to reach the centre of the pyramid and the gold they desperately sought. And unknown to many who tried and failed, they became inflicted by an invisible curse that hung in the air and slowly dissipated their energy levels. According to legend, just as the workers positioned the last stone, the great priests of the time would place a curse at the entrance to the labyrinth.

The curse only became apparent when the robbers, confused and lost in the labyrinth, gave up. As the lights of their burning candles died, so did any ray of hope of reaching the gold or even finding their way back out of the labyrinth. With darkness all around them, all their hope gone and a total sense of despondency engulfing them, the robbers finally realized they'd been breathing the poisoned air. All their initial energy, enthusiasm and eagerness seeped out of them. All that was left to do was lie down and wait for a slow death. They'd become inflicted with the Curse of Dissipating Energy.

Alas, our story doesn't have a happy ending (sorry).

In business today, we are inflicted with the same curse. At the start of any implementation, energy levels are high and people sense the excitement and anticipation of something new. But as the implementation journey rolls out, their energy is often sapped until all that is left is hopelessness and disillusionment.

In summary:

Vision is your dream
Strategy is the driver
Implementaion ensures delivery

- Leaders need to commit more resources, time, effort, planning and consistent energy to the entire journey—the start, middle and finish.

- Break the mold of the last 40 years and realize that in order to succeed, you must go beyond typical implementation.

- Strategy directs leaders what to do. The Implementation Compass makes the strategy come alive.

- Leaders spend too much time creating strategies and initiatives that fail to deliver the anticipated results because of poor implementation.

- Implementation is when leaders must stand up and be counted by taking the action that supports what they have discussed to date.

- If people in organizations know what goes wrong, why do they keep repeating the same mistakes?

- Over the 40 years since strategy implementation first became a topic in business, leaders have failed to make any dramatic improvements to how they approach implementation.

References
[1] Bridges Business Consultancy Int. Pte Ltd 5 year research
[2] Norton, David P. and Robert S. Kaplan, The Balanced Scorecard: Translating Strategy into Action, Harvard Business School Press,
[3] Taking Charge of Change 10 Principles for Managing People and Performance, Douglas K. Smith, Addison Wesley Publishing Co

chapter 2
Implementation
Fundamentals

The Implementation Fundamentals are the basic guidelines to consider when implementing your strategy. They are divided into eight traditional and six new fundamentals. The eight traditional fundamentals draw on the lessons of bygone years and should sound familiar. The six new ones draw on research conducted by Bridges over a five year period. The research, conducted across South East Asia, identifies the state of strategy implementation according to individuals in both multinational and local companies who shared their experiences of putting different strategies in place.

Eight Traditional Fundamentals

1. Communicating the Vision

2. Identifying Obstacles

3. Creating a Sense of Urgency

4. Training

5. Identifying Change Agents

6. Rewarding and Recognizing

7. Setting and Celebrating Milestones

8. Monitoring Success

Six New Fundamentals

1. For the Right Results, Take the Right Action

2. Double the Effort

3. It's not Rocket Science, It's Discipline

4. Controlled Chaos!

5. Theory Promises: Success Sells

6. Constant Review

Eight Traditional Fundamentals

01. Communicating the Vision

For many organizations, implementing strategy starts with sharing the vision across the whole organization. This vision, a description of the future state of the organization, should act as the base on which the strategy is founded and inspire employees to achieve new heights. By leveraging it, leaders can speak positively about the future and provide a solid platform for sharing key activities. The vision is also a rallying call to galvanize staff. (Chapter 6 provides a framework on how your vision can be communicated effectively.)

Bill Gates rallied the people at Microsoft around a vision of "a computer on every desk." Today that may not seem like much of a challenge, but remember, Microsoft was founded more than 25 years ago at a time when most of us did not even know how to use a computer (and were hoping we wouldn't have to learn!). Having fulfilled that vision, today, Microsoft's vision[1] is to *"enable people and businesses throughout the world to realize their full potential"*.

02. Identifying Obstacles

Project yourself into the future. The year you identified for your vision to become a reality has arrived! You are so successful, *Fortune Magazine* has put you on its front cover. Close your eyes for a moment, look at your cover and read the headline, then open your eyes again and write out the headline you saw.

Now, while your mind is still in the future, reflect on all you had to overcome to achieve today's tremendous results. Write down the main obstacles you encountered. Once you've completed your list, bring yourself back to the present and prioritize the obstacles. Now ask yourself, "What do I need to do today to overcome the obstacles I identified?"

This simple exercise is a powerful tool to help leadership teams identify the strategies needed to achieve their desired results. Leaders prepare the organization for the journey ahead by identifying the expected obstacles.

Bridges worked with a financial institution that wanted to counterattack an aggressive move in the market by its closest competitor. Its new strategy was based on creating value using an innovative e-commerce approach.

Before launching this strategy, team members came together from all over the region for one day, to discuss the details. A goal of the meeting was to identify the perceived obstacles, including lack of communication across the group, confusion about roles and responsibilities, budget concerns and client response. They then ranked these obstacles in order of their importance to make the strategy work and most importantly, identified a counter activity to overcome the obstacles. The planning didn't stop there. As follow up, the leaders agreed to review the counter activity every week for the first three months and then every month after that. They wanted to ensure that the strategy was removing the obstacles as planned.

03. Creating a Sense of Urgency

"Why change?" is a question commonly heard by leaders preparing to implement their strategy. One effective response to pre-empt and overcome staff resistance is to create a sense of urgency about the change. (This is discussed in the Biz Case segment in Chapter 5.)

The urgency may be driven by shrinking market share, poor customer satisfaction or poor productivity. The leader provides best–case and worst–case scenarios to create a powerful contrast that will encourage staff to participate and adopt the new strategy. As an example, a property company in Hong Kong wanted to change its leadership style after the new CEO identified that the existing style wouldn't be effective in the 21st Century. The company's current results and financial projections were excellent and the CEO knew that any proposed changes would be questioned and challenged. After all, why fix what wasn't broken?

The CEO, however, conducted some customer research and was horrified to see the poor ratings and feedback customers gave the organization. He also noted the organization's reputation for its lack of response to customer concerns and complaints. Paradoxically, this information provided the needed sense of urgency. The CEO drew a correlation between customer satisfaction and revenue, and demonstrated that customer satisfaction was a lead indicator of profits.

04. Training

On many occasions, implementing a new strategy means teaching the staff new skills. For example, British Airways was transformed into a more customer-centric organization. Everyone on staff participated in a "Putting People First" training. This helped them understand how they could be more customer-centric in their own jobs. The training itself acted as a catalyst that brought about a dramatic improvement in customer satisfaction and market share in a highly competitive industry.

They identified that only eight percent of disgruntled customers complained; 23 percent of those complaints were never recorded and 69 percent of disgruntled customers never complained at all. A one percent increase in positive customer comments led to between £200,000 to £400,000 increase in revenue!

A word of caution here—training is a means to an end. Far too many leaders believe that training is the major part of what they need to do. As a result, little else is done to support the implementation. Consequently, the implementation fails more often than not. Remember, training supports implementation; it is frequently not the solution in itself.

In the 1990s, when Reuters was expanding quickly across Asia Pacific, Country Manager Francis Tan recognized a need to respond to employee feedback. Staff members complained about a lack of communication between divisions. As the organization was growing so fast, not enough time was being committed to staff growth. Mr. Tan worked with his human resource manager to identify the training needed and the best provider for it. Every staff member then attended a two-day offsite training. In addition, Mr. Tan personally attended the closing of every session to demonstrate his commitment and sincerity to the training process and organize other activities to support the training. Reuters has gone on to successfully grow across the region.

A word of caution: Training is a means to an end, not the end in itself.

05. Identifying Change Agents

Change Agents are staff members who willingly step up to the responsibility of implementation without being asked. They respond positively and enthusiastically to the challenges ahead. In this book, we refer to them as *Mavericks*.

Because Mavericks drive change in every organization, it is critical that you can identify who these people are and encourage and support them as they lead the implementation through action. (Chapter 4 explains how your staff will respond during the implementation and the specific role of Mavericks.)

In the movie *Sister Act*, Whoopi Goldberg plays a Las Vegas dancer who walks in on her boyfriend just as he shoots someone. The police want her to testify. To ensure that she is safe from her now ex-boyfriend, they hide her in the last place anyone would look for her—a nunnery. At one point Mother Superior sends Sister Mary Clarence (aka Deloris—Whoopi's character) to join the choir as a punishment for breaking the rules. The choir needs a drastic change. As one of the nuns declares, "We're terrible."

Before long, choir members recognize that Sister Mary Clarence has singing skills and ask her to help them. As Sister Mary Clarence transforms the choir, she identifies a Change Agent in Sister Mary Patrick. Full of enthusiasm and energy, Sister Mary Patrick provides the support and drive to assist in the transformation of the choir; Sister Mary Patrick is a born Maverick.

06. Rewarding and Recognizing

As your employees start to adopt the new implementation, make sure they're supported and encouraged to continue demonstrating the desired behaviors by being rewarded (financial kudos) and recognized (non-financial kudos) for their efforts. If they don't receive rewards or recognition, they will likely stop the new behaviors and revert to the old way of doing things. If your staff works the old way, then you'll get the same old results. (Chapter 12 looks at what you can do to recognize your staff members and encourage them to adopt the required new behaviors.)

A high performance culture can only be achieved by truly paying for performance. This requires a genuine willingness to significantly differentiate pay for poor, average and exceptional performers and an equal willingness to communicate these performance outcomes in a forthright and transparent manner to all employees.

Dharma Chandran, General Manager,
Performance Management & Rewards, Westpac Bank

Need a simple way to encourage staff to participate? Pass out teddy bears! In one organization, every time people demonstrated a specific behavior, they received a small teddy bear that was proudly displayed on top of the computer screen. Others walking by could see immediately who'd been awarded the most bears. The competition to have many bears on display became a fun challenge. As a result, desired behaviors were demonstrated frequently. This program succeeded partly because it was offered for only a limited time.

07. Setting and Celebrating Milestones

Celebrate successes to create a positive environment. Find an excuse to celebrate early on, then keep celebrating. As you start out on your implementation, leaders need to build momentum and excitement to encourage others to get involved. Be sure to set milestones to provide targets for the group and break down the steps needed for successful implementation.

During the implementation phase, leaders may be confused about what to focus on. Milestones provide the sign posts that guide everyone through the implementation. Celebrating the achievement of these milestones adds to building the momentum and excitement.

Sam Walton the founder of Wal-Mart really knew how to celebrate milestones. Pessimistic that the company would not make its projected pretax profit of more than eight percent, Sam Walton made a bet with his colleague, David Glass—if Wal-Mart met its target, he would show up on Wall Street wearing a grass skirt and dancing the hula. Well, Sam Walton lost his wager. And David Glass recorded the entire spectacle which was then shown at the next management meeting. He also notified the press and the event became a hallmark in Wal-Mart's history.

You want to keep your staff members excited about your implementation but setting milestones with just the right distance between them is tough to call.

Once you've initiated the implementation, track, adjust and celebrate your milestones.

08. Monitoring Success

Keep track of how you're doing throughout the implementation process. Monitor your success to ensure you're achieving the milestones. Be prepared to adjust your strategy if required.

What you pay attention to is what your staff will pay attention to. Conversely, if you stop monitoring the implementation and take your eye off the ball, so will your staff.

Knowledge is power, as Eddie Cheever reminded everyone after winning the 1998 Indianapolis 500. Cheever believes the key to success is to keep the team informed. The information sharing lessons from the Indy 500 can be applied to managing change in organizations: the team monitors every second of the race through 30 sensors built into the car. After every race, the team debriefs, leaving everyone with more knowledge than they'd started with. "The wining team is the one that makes best use of that knowledge," Cheever says.

Research Results–
creation of the Six New
Fundamentals

The basis for creating the six new fundamentals comes from three sources:

1. The Bridges survey carried out over a five year period
2. Secondary research
3. Bridges' experience from clients

The following highlights the research results from the Bridges' survey of leaders in South East Asian companies.

Survey Details

Over a five year period, Bridges interviewed over 150 line managers from various industries to identify the state of strategy implementation in South East Asia.

Two-thirds of the organizations surveyed employ more than 10,000 people. Key industries represented in the survey were energy, utilities and government bodies. One-third of the interviewees were senior managers and two-thirds were middle managers. In the survey, the word implementation was replaced with change because change is a commonly accepted word in business, while implementation is not as familiar.

State of the South East Asia Region

The two most common change initiatives implemented by organizations in the survey are the **Balanced Scorecard** and **Vision, Mission** and **Values.**

These are followed by **New Corporate Strategy** and **ISO.**

Almost one-third of the change initiatives were scheduled for completion within 12 months and were actually completed within the timeframe, although they didn't deliver the desired results largely due to a lack of support and action from people in the organization, poor communication and overwhelming resistance from staff.

Key Findings

The findings from the survey are both startling and thought provoking.
They overwhelmingly show that the three most difficult challenges faced by managers and staff in implementing change in their organizations are:

1. Gaining support and action
2. Communicating the change
3. Overcoming resistance from staff

The Top 10 Challenges in Implementing change Initiatives

Ranking	Challenge
1	Gaining support and action
2	Communicating the change
3	Overcoming resistance from staff
4	Support of senior management
5	Aligning processes
6	Tracking success of implementation
7	Changing rewards and recognition
8	Acquiring customer feedback
9	Implementing new technology
10	Acquiring budget

(© Bridges, 2005)

Gaining Support and Action

The survey pinpointed the number-one reason for change failure is *lack of support and action from the people in the organization.* It showed that people don't change either the way they work or the way they think about their work, possibly because both staff and managers suffer from change fatigue. In the last few years of management practice, we've witnessed a plethora of change initiatives: CRM (Customer Relationship Management); Six Sigma; Vision-Mission-Values; ERP (Enterprise Resource Planning); Balanced Scorecard; ISO; Customer Service; Core Competencies; Total Quality Management...the list just keeps growing.

As a result, staff and managers have become battle weary, tired of being "called to arms" too often and too soon following the latest initiative.

Earlier research showed that change initiatives failed because of a lack of support from top management. In the Bridges survey, however, this reason ranked fourth on the list. The findings suggest that the difficulty lies more in gaining support *from across the organization, not just from senior management.*

This result has possibly dropped from number one to number four because senior managers have repeatedly heard that if change is going to succeed, they must get personally involved. From our experience, it seems they have finally taken that message to heart.

Alternatively, it is possible that leaders see the need for gaining support, taking action, communicating change and overcoming resistance as *even more important* than having a commitment from top management.

Communicating the Change

According to the Bridges survey, the most common vehicle for communicating change initiatives to the staff was via email (25 percent of the time) followed by briefings and newsletters. Only five percent of those interviewed felt that staff members clearly understood their roles after hearing or reading about a change initiative. This tends to show that while email is a useful means of communication, it is not strong enough to stand on its own, even when it is complemented with briefings and newsletters.

The survey also revealed that most communication was front-loaded—too much information and activity at the start, closely followed by a lack of consistent communication strategy over the term of the initiative or implementation.

Staff members resist change when they don't clearly understand why it's being adopted and what they're supposed to do. Staff resistance was more apparent in cases where the change wasn't communicated well.

People simply didn't know what they were supposed to do.

The greatest resistance in the organizations came from middle managers—54 percent versus 13 percent from top management and 23 percent from front-line people. This surprising conclusion reinforces the importance of involving middle managers in the change process and communicating effectively with them and through them.

Middle managers are sometimes referred to as the *thermal layer* of an organization because they absorb many of the key initiatives being driven through the organization and strongly influence actions taken. For this reason, it is important for leaders to work closely with middle managers, providing guidance and encouragement, and articulating reasons for implementing the new strategy.

THIS WORKS!

Leaders in the organization must act as coaches and guides, encouraging middle managers through the change initiative.

Other Results

90 percent of change initiatives fail to deliver the desired results stated by the management at the outset of the change initiative.

97 percent of the people interviewed agreed with the statement "Implementation fails because of bad execution, not bad strategy."

20 percent of the changes lasted three to five years.

60 percent of the changes were driven by local initiatives, 20 percent by regional and 20 percent by global.

Some of the most common top-line views on why change initiatives failed were:

- **Lack of commitment from top management to enforce the strategies**
- **No follow through**
- **Resource constraints**
- **Change of leadership**
- **No clear directions and purpose conveyed to staff at all levels**
- **Constantly changing performance indicators**
- **Changing priorities**

The Benefit of Hindsight

With the benefit of hindsight, here is what survey respondents said they would do differently if they were to implement the same strategy or initiative again:

- **Obtain total commitment from top management**
- **Act fast**
- **Communicate aggressively**
- **Identify champions/leaders (Mavericks)**
- **Give all staff members a clear idea of the changes to be made**
- **Determine clear targets (benefits for employee) and communicate them through the whole organization**
- **Clearly identify top management as the driving force**
- **Increase emphasis on developing an action plan**

Six New Fundamentals

The six new fundamentals of implementation evolved from the research including and beyond the Bridges survey. These new fundamentals complement and support the eight traditional fundamentals. By adopting both the traditional and the new fundamentals, leaders dramatically increase the organization's chances for a successful strategy implementation.

"Of course we will do the right thing!"

1. For the Right Results, Take the Right Action

Taking the *right action* is the catalyst that moves organizations from strategy creation to strategy implementation.

The *right action* is the progression of action steps you need to take to create the right results.

When implementing a strategy, it is critical to know from the outset *what* and *what not* to focus on and to identify what it takes to transform the people and processes. Generally, this isn't done well by leaders, partly because strategy creation absorbs a lot of their time and energy. Once the creation is complete, leaders tend to consider the hardest part over and fail to focus on implementation.

To implement strategy successfully, identify the actions needed, then follow through during the whole implementation.

Often, during the implementation phase, staff are bombarded by competing activities demanding their attention simultaneously. By establishing a structured action plan up front, you can remove this confusion—an action plan will help staff identify what they *should* be doing and communicate to them the reason for taking action—and the desired results.

This will ensure you're doing the right thing!

"Hang on," you might say, "of course we will do the right thing." Maybe you will, but more often than not, part of the reason strategy implementations fail to deliver the results is because as the implementation rolls out, leaders and staff get distracted or discouraged and lose focus. Once focus is lost, there is a risk that actions taken will not be aimed at delivering the results. Unfortunately, leaders or staff may be paying lip service to the implementation and taking actions that just make them look good in front of the boss, but fail to have any impact.

Implementation without the right action is like expecting to win the lottery without buying a ticket. It's like planning to get fit without exercising or expecting to improve your golf game without practicing.

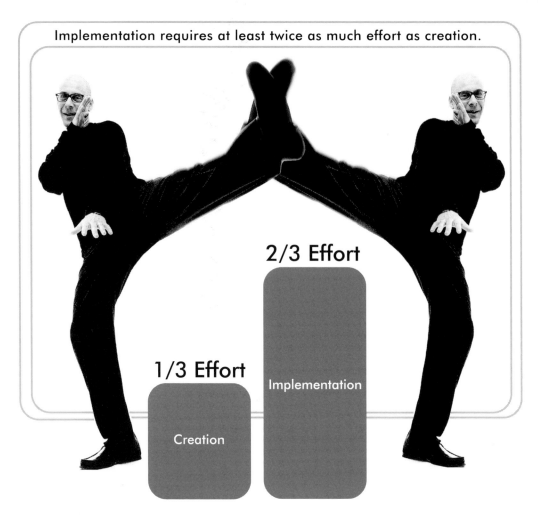

Implementation requires at least twice as much effort as creation.

2/3 Effort

1/3 Effort

Implementation

Creation

2. Double the Effort

It takes at least twice the effort to implement strategy as it does to create it. The second new fundamental of implementation is that whatever time, resources, effort and energy it took to create your strategy, you will need to at least double it for successful implementation.

Why? Creating the strategy typically involves only the top management, while implementation involves the whole organization. When creating the strategy, the organization had only one level of managers to deal with; now leaders have several. When creating the strategy, you needed resources only for the leadership team; now you must cater to everyone.

Successful implementation involves:

- Having the Right People
- In the Right Place
- At the Right Time

Success requires allocating the right amount of time, resources, effort and energy to the implementation plan.

The importance implementation plays in ensuring success and the need to increase the implementation effort is only just beginning to be recognized. Leaders still place their main focus on strategy creation.

The next time you are in a bookshop, go to the section on management strategy and browse through the selection of books. Most, if not all, will tell you what strategy is and how to create it.

But what about its implementation?

What good is a strategy if it's not implemented successfully?

Start to shift from strategy creation toward implementation. (Another good reference is *Execution: The Discipline of Getting Things Done* by Larry Bossidy and Ram Charan.) If you're tired of poor implementation results, start giving it the attention it requires.

3. It's not Rocket Science,
it's Discipline

Successful implementation is not complex but it does require discipline—the discipline to do the things you're supposed to do when you need to do them and to keep on doing them until you achieve the right results.

It's like healthy living. We know that a healthy lifestyle is good for us, yet most people do not exercise enough and do not eat the right food. Bruce Nordstrom, head of Nordstrom's, the U.S. clothing retailer, was asked why Nordstrom's is so successful. He replied, "We do not do anything different; we just do what we are supposed to do."

Successful implementation means being disciplined to:

- Identify the structured actions and follow them through to completion
- Align the organization's culture toward desired results
- Align the work processes toward desired results
- Maintain management support
- Communicate throughout the organization frequently
- Measure actions
- Recognize and reward staff for demonstrating desired behaviors
- Constantly review actions

Execution is not just tactics—it is a discipline and a system.
Larry Bossidy and Ram Charan

Implementation takes discipline to ensure that the right results are achieved.

Based on a five-year study, Joyce and Robinson Nohira[2], in their article "What Really Works" *(Harvard Business Review July 2003)* state that embracing CRM, ERP or something similar does not necessarily catapult you to the head of your industry. What really counts is the *disciplined attention to operations.*

That means that once you have completed your strategy creation and identified the structured actions, you must adopt the discipline to follow through on the actions until the results are achieved.

4. Controlled Chaos!

Staff must work both the old way and the new way simultaneously while there is chaos all around them.

The basics of Change Management 101 say that before making a change, an organization must be taken out of equilibrium and into chaos and then back into equilibrium. During this transitional stage, everyone has to deal with the chaos that follows and minimize the disturbance period—the period when the organization is in chaos and staff members are unsure about what to focus on and what is important as they move forward.

During this disturbance period, they must work both in the old way and the new. They still need to follow the old systems, structures and standards while learning and adopting new ways of working. While that is happening, leaders are working to move the organization back to equilibrium as quickly as possible while providing guidance through the chaos.

Here's an example—a sales team goes about its business every day selling the organization's products. Management becomes aware that their leading revenue product is reaching the end of its product life cycle, so it introduces a new product for the sales team to sell. At the point of introducing the new product, does the sales team immediately stop selling the old product?

No, of course not. There is still a market for the old product and customers are still buying it. The organization must have a strategy to sell both the old product and the new product simultaneously. This is an example of both old and new in action.

Preparing for the chaos of change takes place while following old ways of working and adopting new ones.

A transitional period takes the organization from working the old way to the new way. This period (described in Chapter 8) can last from two weeks to two years, depending on the objectives of the strategy. Far too often, organizations charge forward without considering how staff members will handle the strategy and without preparing them for it. Getting ready for chaos minimizes the disturbance to the business and staff and increases the chances of success.

5. Theory Promises: Success Sells

It's easier to "sell" a success than a theory.

When setting out to implement your strategy, you will want staff members to join in but how do you convince them? You can tell them what the benefits will be for them (e.g., shorter working hours, larger bonuses) but some may have heard such promises before and doubt the sincerity of them. They may have experienced implementations that did not deliver in their previous organizations, or they may have heard the same spiel from a previous CEO who failed to deliver on the promise. Whatever the reason, many people are skeptical when they hear their leaders announcing promises linked to a new strategy. After all, it is the employees who take on extra work, deal with disruptions and make the strategy come alive. The leaders don't implement strategy, they only create it. When translated into the language of the staff, all this adds up to only one thing—*more work*.

To convince them to support the implementation, show them a success, not a theory, by sponsoring a pilot project in aid of the implementation. Position it where you have the most opportunity for success. Let it provide the opportunity to test out your theory and see it in action. During the pilot project, provide all the attention and support required to ensure success. Once it's complete, you'll have a success story you can share with the staff to show that the strategy works. In addition, those who participated in the pilot can share their positive experiences with others and help them.

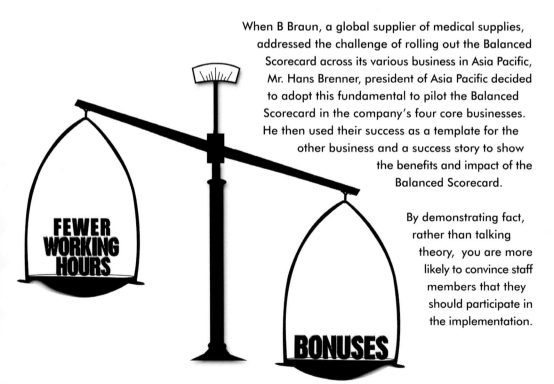

When B Braun, a global supplier of medical supplies, addressed the challenge of rolling out the Balanced Scorecard across its various business in Asia Pacific, Mr. Hans Brenner, president of Asia Pacific decided to adopt this fundamental to pilot the Balanced Scorecard in the company's four core businesses. He then used their success as a template for the other business and a success story to show the benefits and impact of the Balanced Scorecard.

By demonstrating fact, rather than talking theory, you are more likely to convince staff members that they should participate in the implementation.

FEWER WORKING HOURS

BONUSES

6. Constant Review

It's only when you constantly review the implementation of your strategy that you reinforce its importance and demonstrate the commitment needed to overcome numerous obstacles.

Implementing strategy requires tremendous effort that needs to be coordinated to achieve the desired results. To ensure this happens, leaders must constantly review the actions being taken.

Although this may not sound like a startling revelation, it's one of the most powerful actions leadership can take but probably one of the weakest among leaders today.

Very often, focus is placed at the start of implementation, a buzz of activity starts up and everyone's fired up. After a while though, enthusiasm dwindles and activities lose steam. Holding constant reviews will ensure your staff members are taking the actions they're supposed to take to produce the right results and so maintain the momentum.

Employees pay attention to what leaders pay attention to. Holding constant reviews will keep everyone focused on the implementation.

At a Typical Review, the Leader will ask:

- What are the deliverables?
- What has changed in the strategic landscape?
- Are we achieving the Critical Success Factors (CSF)?
- What lessons have we learned from both successes and failures?
- What is our next step?

When you have a detailed implementation strategy, then you are ready to start your journey through the maze of implementation.

The Maze

Implementing strategy is similar to finding your way through a maze.

The metaphor of the maze reflects the effort that people must make. Implementation involves taking many turns down an indistinct path and overcoming the obstacles and challenges to complete their implementation. It also reflects the excitement that is typical at the start of a new adventure and the dissipation of the energy over time.

Implementation is like finding your way through a maze.

COMPLETING THE MAZE	COMPLETING THE IMPLEMENTATION PLAN
There are different mazes of different size, complexity and length.	Each organization's implementation maze is different and unique. Although you can copy some best practices, the organization must find its own path.
At the beginning, people are determined to find a way through the maze. No one plans to give up.	At the start of implementing a new strategy, everyone plans for success but most strategies fail to deliver the desired results.
At the entrance to the maze you stop to review the challenge you are embarking on.	Management must communicate to everyone the reasons for the new strategy and explain the benefits as well as the actions everyone must take.
People react differently to the challenge of finding their way through the maze.	You must know your team and focus your attention on the staff who will take action.
As you journey through the maze you will make many wrong turns because no one has a map.	When you implement an strategy, you plan for the future but no one knows what will happen. When actions fail to create the right outcome, you learn from taking the wrong turn to make sure you do not repeat the mistake.
You need signposts for the journey so that you do not lose your bearings.	In implementation, you need a scorecard to tell you if you are moving in the right direction and achieving your desired results.
When making a wrong turn, realize it's a learning opportunity. Likewise, when you find the right path, celebrate the success.	A leader's role is to point employees in the right direction and then motivate them along the way. When staff members are ready to give up, the leader invigorates them. When someone does something right, leaders should recognize and reward them.
When you find the right path, you must let everyone who's with you know the right path too.	The organization must get aligned behind the initiative. The culture, processes and day-to-day actions should all be focused in the right direction.
You need to make sure everyone is following the right path.	Along the way, you must constantly review your progress to make sure you are heading in the right direction, learning from mistakes, achieving the desired results and seeing that the rest of the organization is moving in the same direction.
When you complete the maze, celebrate your success.	Upon completing the maze, celebrate your success but also start preparing for the next maze. It's just around the corner.

He who every morning plans the transactions of the day and follows out that plan carries a thread that will guide them through the maze of the most busy life. But where no plan is laid, where the disposal of time is surrendered merely to the chance of incidence, chaos will soon reign.

Victor Hugo

Going Down the Wrong Path

When wandering around in a maze, it's easy to take the wrong path. When implementing your strategy, you will be faced with many decisions to make and the right path to take won't always be obvious. In the maze, you know when you have gone down the wrong path because you come to a dead end. Unfortunately, in business the signs are not always so visible. By the time you realize that you are on the wrong path it may be too late. (In Chapter 7, we'll look at the importance of measurement to guide you through the difficult journey ahead. In Chapter 13, we'll look at the importance of constantly reviewing your journey. Both of these practices will help ensure that you can adjust your direction before it's too late.)

There is one more vital element to be aware of—other people may lead you down the wrong path…unintentionally and sometimes intentionally.

When implementing a new strategy, the organization and the people will go through changes. There will be a high level of activity and discussion, especially at the start of the implementation. Inevitably, some people will take up your time and distract you from your true path while others may intentionally sabotage you.

WATCH OUT!
Sometimes others will lead you down the wrong path—intentionally or unintentionally.

Many people think of execution as detail work, that it's below the dignity of business leaders. I think that it's the leader's most important job.

Larry Johnston, CEO

Strategy is about deciding what to do, execution is about getting it done. Both are essential skills for a modern leader.

McKinsey & Company

Implementation is not a frontal attack, you must bombard the company.

David Norton

To transform an organization there must be a wholesale shifting of resources from what was appropriate for the old ideas of the business to what is appropriate for the new.

Peter Drucker

The best is the enemy of the good. By this I mean that a good plan violently executed now is better than a perfect plan next week.

General George S. Patton, Jr.

Accept that you will either pay for getting what you want (commitment) or you will pay for not getting what you want (resistance) and the payments may come early or late – but change is expensive and you will pay.

Daryl Conner

The only constant today is change.

Heracleitus, 2500 years ago

The hardest thing to learn in life is which bridges to cross and which to burn.

David Russel

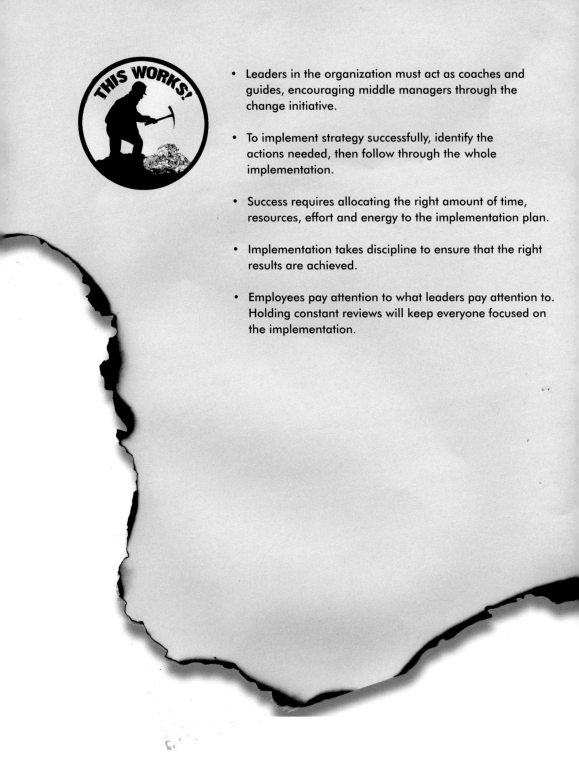

THIS WORKS!

- Leaders in the organization must act as coaches and guides, encouraging middle managers through the change initiative.

- To implement strategy successfully, identify the actions needed, then follow through the whole implementation.

- Success requires allocating the right amount of time, resources, effort and energy to the implementation plan.

- Implementation takes discipline to ensure that the right results are achieved.

- Employees pay attention to what leaders pay attention to. Holding constant reviews will keep everyone focused on the implementation.

- A word of caution – training is a means to an end, not the end in itself.

- You want to keep your staff members excited about your change agenda but setting milestones with just the right distance between them is tough to call.

- Implementation without the right action is like expecting to win the lottery without buying a ticket. It's like planning to get fit without exercising or expecting to improve your golf game without practicing.

- Preparing for the chaos of change takes place while following old ways of working and adopting new ones.

- Sometimes others will lead you down the wrong path—intentionally or unintentionally!

References
[1] Dated June, 2003, at www.microsoft.com
[2] Nohira, Joyce and Robinson, "What Really Works" Harvard Business Review, July 2003, pg 46

To Understand the Essence of this Chapter, Solve the following Riddle:

Five birds sit on a fence and three decide to leave.

How many birds are left on the fence? Is it none, two or five?

Consider this for a moment.

The answer is

chapter 3

Want the Right Results?
Take the Right Action

You build a bridge one brick at a time.

You get though the implementation maze by taking the right action—one action after another in the right direction to create the right results.

In this chapter, we will look at the intricate challenge of taking the right action to drive your strategy through your organization.

Why is the anwser to the riddle 5?

Because the birds discussed what needed to be done at their three-day offsite meeting. They developed a strategy on how to leave. They chatted about the benefits of flying off and had numerous conference calls but continued to sit on that fence because they did not take...*action*.

It's action that moves people (and birds) from where they are to where they want to go. It's the *right* action that moves an organization from where it is to where it needs to go.

> Implementation is all about taking the right action:
> # You need to walk, not just talk.
> # Decide, don't just reside.
> # Act, don't just react.

To find your way through the implementation maze, take the right action.

Of the organizations we have studied, the top 10 percent of those who have achieved successful implementations commonly take action around the key areas that will impact their results. They're led by people who focus on actions that will have the greatest impact on the end result. To be successful, the leaders of these companies don't rush blindly into the maze; they prepare for the journey, knowing specifically what they need to do. Then they do it and follow up to make sure they are obtaining the right results.

Too often, leaders of organizations don't clearly visualize the destination. In reality, the bar of expectations frequently gets lowered along the way and anticipated results change.

While the exact details will vary by company and effort, the chief reason most change efforts fail is that they are directed at design as opposed to "do." The effort is very often one of articulating the change you want to bring about rather than actually doing it.[1]

Douglas K. Smith

Focus on the actions that will have the greatest impact on the right results.

As you embark on your journey through the maze, you'll be required to take many actions. Some will be time-consuming and will result in low returns. Others will be blind alleys in the maze that are, in reality, will take you further away from your destination.

To identify the right action, ask yourself these three fundamental questions:

1

What results define success for the implementation?

2

How will we know we are achieving the right results?

3

What actions need to be taken to achieve these results?

1. What Results Define Success for the Implementation?

Let's take a closer look at this first question because it has many inner meanings.

When implementing strategy, many leaders take action. But instead of advancing the organization in the right direction, their actions turn out to be detrimental to the results.

To avoid negative results, first identify the right results (goals or outcomes) so you can give purpose to the implementation before you take action.

Too often, leaders of organizations don't clearly visualize the destination.

Know Where You're Going

Before starting out on your journey, know your destination and the landmarks that will allow you to recognize when you are "on course" and when you have arrived. Clearly paint a picture of your destination and articulate the milestones to be reached along the way.

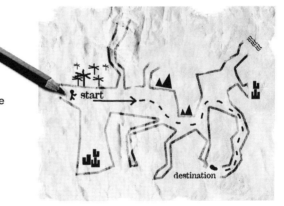

In reality, the bar of expectations frequently gets lowered along the way and the expected results change.

"Would you tell me please, which way I ought to go from here?"
"That depends a good deal on where you want to get to," said the Cat.
"I don't much care where..." said Alice.
"Then it doesn't matter which way you go," said the Cat.
"... so long as I get somewhere," Alice added as an explanation.
"Oh, you're sure to do that," said the Cat, "if you only walk enough."

Lewis Carroll, Alice in Wonderland

Make the strategy come alive by taking the right action and making the organization's success everyone's success.

Bridges was assisting a multinational company in Asia Pacific in implementing its global strategy in the region. The people in U.S. head office articulated why the strategy had been adopted and what needed to be done and had created the strategy from a global perspective. The leaders in the Asian Pacific countries were not sure what was expected from them and how this global strategy affected their actions. Therefore, they had to first define the right result for Asia Pacific and then work with each of the country teams to define success for all of them.

Beware of Becoming Over Focused

Organizations that spend too much time perfecting their strategies miss opportunities. When they finally get going, they discover that conditions have changed and they need to adjust, or even completely change the strategy.

Bridges came to the rescue of one company that had become so absorbed in defining the destination and the strategy that it hadn't started on the journey. The company had spent large amounts of money researching and developing its new strategy, but faced having nothing to show except a large, well-researched and beautifully bound document.

Bridges helped put the vision of the destination strongly in place and worked with the leaders of this organization to make the strategy come alive by quickly defining actions and kick-starting the strategy.

Before starting on an implementation, the leaders must have the fundamentals of the strategy in place along with a clearly defined vision and a plan of action. As an organization enters the maze of implementation, its leaders will find out soon enough if the strategy is working and where it needs to change its course.

Beware! Some organizations become consumed with defining the destination and wait too long to take action.

2. What Actions do We need to take to Achieve the Right Results?

After having identified what will define success, carefully note the right actions that will deliver the right results. Actions aren't random, uncoordinated activities; they are coordinated, focused and planned to move the organization down the right path of the maze. They can be identified by knowing where your organization is going and what it will take to get to its destination.

That doesn't sound too hard but, alas, the challenge is in doing what you're supposed to do when you're supposed to do it.

Also, the actions each organization has to take are unique because each implementation maze is different.

Consider taking action in these areas:

Communications
Measurement
People
Culture
Process
Reward and Recognition
Reviews

You'll read more about each of these areas throughout the book.

How will We know we are Achieving the Desired Results?

When implementing strategy, employees sometimes feel that their boss has asked them to find their way through the maze blindfolded. No signposts exist to direct them and they receive no feedback to correct their performance. Consequently, they stumble forward as if walking in the dark.

To guide them towards the action steps, it's important to incorporate the right measures and reviews. Just as a compass shows them direction, "measures" guide them through the implementation maze while "review" tells them how they're performing.

Integrate "measures" to guide you through the maze and "reviews" to give you feedback on performance.

In the last ten years, measurement in organizations has dramatically improved due to the introduction of the Balanced Scorecard, a management tool for implementing strategy. An estimated 50 percent of Fortune 500 companies have adopted this Scorecard. It makes managing the strategy more tangible while setting measurable goals for everyone in the organization and ensuring alignment between the desired strategic results and day-to-day activities.

Reviewing action allows experiences and lessons learned to be shared, as well as correcting mistakes and celebrating achievements. Remember, this often-ignored discipline can make the difference between success and failure.

Your organization's review can be as simple as asking these five key questions:

1. What is going well?
2. What do we need to do differently?
3. What needs to be changed?
4. What has changed externally?
5. What have we learned?

Before starting to take action, ensure you are doing everything possible to succeed and make sure the whole team reaches the end of the maze. After initiating the implementation, constantly review it to make sure you're achieving the right results.

The mechanics for conducting the implementation review are found in Chapter 13. But first, let's look at the philosophy of action—what's needed to take the right action.

The Philosophy of Action

The philosophy of action considers the different elements involved before, during and after the action is taken and helps ensure that you're setting staff up to succeed. Too often, organizations ask staff members to change without providing the right tools or support. So make sure they're prepared to take action and are given the right support during the implementation.

Cambridge Dictionary defines:
Action (noun): The process of doing something, or something done, especially for a particular purpose.

Ensuring staff members are prepared to take the right action involves eight elements:

1. Result
2. Attitude
3. Knowledge
4. Skills
5. Action
6. Reinforcement
7. Result
8. Feedback

READY? for 8 elements

KEY QUESTIONS	ELEMENT	SOURCE
WHAT DO WE WANT TO ACHIEVE?	**RESULT**	SENIOR MANAGEMENT
WHAT DOES THE ORGANIZATION NEED TO CHANGE IN ITS THINKING?	**ATTITUDE**	VALUES & BELIEFS
WHAT DO WE NOT KNOW TODAY THAT WE NEED TO KNOW FOR TOMORROW?	**KNOWLEDGE**	RESEARCH AND ANALYSIS
WHAT COMPETENCIES DO WE NEED?	**SKILLS**	COURSES AND ON THE JOB TRAINING
WHAT ACTION DO WE NEED TO TAKE?	**ACTION**	YOURSELF, AS YOU ARE PERSONALLY RESPONSIBL
WHAT RECOGNITION IS THERE?	**REINFORCEMENT**	IMMEDIATE SUPERVISOR
WHAT IS THE IMPACT—POSITIVE, NEGATIVE OR NO CHANGE?	**RESULT**	CUSTOMER/MARKET/P&
HOW CAN WE CONTINUE TO IMPROVE ON THE ACTION TAKEN?	**FEEDBACK**	IMMEDIATE SUPERVISOR

1 Result

The first step in preparing to take action is to know the end result, just as Stephen Covey said in ***The 7 Habits of Highly Effective People***[2]: "Begin with the end in mind."

The leadership team considers, debates and determines what defines success. Together, you must know where you want to go before starting out, then share the goal with everyone in the organization and inspire staff to achieve it.

2 Attitude

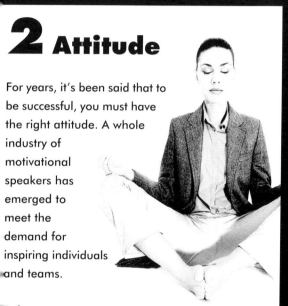

For years, it's been said that to be successful, you must have the right attitude. A whole industry of motivational speakers has emerged to meet the demand for inspiring individuals and teams.

Before you start on your implementation process, become familiar with your organization's attitude by asking yourself, 'Will our current thinking achieve the right results?" If the answer is no, then ask, "What needs to change in our thinking?"

Changing a person's attitude is never easy; it's easier to hire someone who has the right attitude but lacks the right skills than someone with the right skills who lacks the right attitude. It's easier to teach skills than change attitudes. (Influencing the attitudes of staff members is discussed in Chapter 9.)

3 Knowledge

We live in a knowledge economy. Many successful strategies result from having more reliable information than our competitors—and receiving it sooner. This is by no means an innovative strategy, as the following story shows.

When the British first acquired Hong Kong in 1841, it took up to three months for ships to sail from Great Britain to the island. The ships would bring eagerly awaited news from the homeland and trading prices fluctuated depending on whether the news was good or bad. Jardines, the most successful and largest trading house at the time, posted a lookout on the highest hill (today called The Peak) to watch for the arriving ships. They would then dispatch a small boat to intercept the ships and get the news from home before anyone else. Armed with this advance knowledge, Jardines was able to pre-empt the market and beat the competition.

What knowledge do you need that you don't have today?

4 Skills

Implementing change often requires people to work differently. As well as having the right attitude and knowledge, they need training in any new skills they require in their jobs.

Typically, staff members receive training in the core skills needed, but how often are they trained in the skills for tomorrow, the skills needed for implementing the strategy? These might include project management, process redesign, new technology, service and sales, to name just a few.

Let's consider an example from the hospitality industry, which demonstrates the four elements required before taking action—

The **result** for sommeliers (wine waiters) might be to provide excellent service. To do so, they must first have the right **attitude**—a customer-first mindset. They also need **knowledge** of different wines, the ability to recommend the right wine for a given meal and the language for describing the wine to the customer. Good sommeliers have the **skill** to serve the wine deftly—decanting the bottle of red wine over a naked flame, leaving the sediment behind and neatly pouring samples for customers to taste.

5 Action

Nike coined the phrase that epitomizes this element—**just do it**. Enough talk, meetings, retreats and emails—now is the time to take the right action to achieve the right results.

Conditions are never right. People who delay actions until all factors are favorable do nothing.
William Feather

Unfortunately, this quote is still as true today as it was when it was first spoken over a hundred years ago. Inaction or inertia is still the enemy of progress.

You might ask: "But what happens if, in a rush to take action, I get it wrong?" Is it better to take the wrong action than never act at all? As long as you have clearly articulated the fundamentals and the right result, you'll realize (through measurement and reviews) what's working and what isn't, then correct the actions along the way.

Remember, there will always be something you haven't considered that may force you to change your actions and make the added time you've spent planning obsolete.

You should also ask: "Who needs to take the action?" The answer is: "Everyone in the organization." Each person must declare **I am responsible for the change**. Because the majority of the people in the organization are frontline staff, it is therefore mostly frontline workers who make the strategy come alive. Management may create the strategy but every employee lives it as the following story illustrates.

Inaction or inertia is still the enemy of progress

In 1961, John F. Kennedy shared his vision for the space age with the American people: "I believe that this nation should commit itself to achieving the goal, before this decade is out, of landing a man on the moon and returning him safely to the earth."

This short sentence became a vision that inspired the American people in the race against the Russians to have the first man on the moon. The last part of the sentence was also very important to the astronauts!

To find out the effect the President's vision had on the space agency, NASA, a reporter visited its HQ. He noticed that all the engineers and scientists were working at a frantic pace. What impressed the reporter the most, however, was a janitor sweeping the floor.

He stopped to ask the janitor, "What are you doing here?" The janitor stood up straight, looked the reporter directly in the eye and said, "I am helping to put a man on the moon."

JFK's vision was so powerful that it also inspired the frontline workers.

Everyone in the organization must say, "I am responsible for the change."

At the end of the day, success comes from individuals at the front line of operations.

Brian Baker, President of Mobil North America Marketing and Refining

The frontline is the bottomline.

Stephen Covey

Focus on the people in your organization and lead the different groups in the way they respond to change. Keep asking: **"What are you contributing today to make the change happen?"**

Ask yourself "What am I contributing today to make change a reality in my organization?"

The goal, mindset, knowledge and skills prepare you for taking the right action. The next three elements—reinforcement, results and feedback—happen after the action is taken.

6 Reinforcement

Reinforcement encourages staff to keep the initiative moving forward. It can take the form of bonuses, incentives or simple thank-you cards. People respond to positive reinforcement and assurance that they're doing the right thing and that their work is adding value.

Men will die for ribbons.

Napoleon Bonaparte

Napoleon's quote emphasizes that people seek recognition for the work they do. In business today, organizations hand out pins, cards, certificates and prizes as the equivalent of a ribbon.

Leaders have a responsibility to ensure that staff members feel their efforts are recognized and appreciated. Especially important are the early adopters of the implementation—they must feel their efforts are worthwhile and that they're doing the right thing by receiving positive recognition. To sustain the success of the implementation, however, recognition needs to be present through the whole journey.

Recognize staff members who adopt the implementation early. One of the best forms of recognition comes from a person's immediate supervisor saying two simple words—thank you.

7 Results

Are the actions you're taking creating the right results? Leaders tend to charge into an implementation and when asked how it's going, reply "Okay." When asked for evidence to support this, what often comes back is a blank expression. Staff members say, "Evidence? What evidence?"

Successful implementation requires regular regimented reviews that foster changes to be made along the way, rather than a post-mortem after an implementation has failed.

An Asian manufacturer had embarked on an aggressive regional strategy that went extremely well and delivered the right results. Bridges had an opportunity to meet the CEO. When asked what had contributed to the organization's success, he replied, "Keeping track of what we were doing in each country and the flexibility of the management team to respond when required both contributed."

8 Feedback

While reviews provide information at an organizational level, feedback provides personal information on an individual's performance. This means more than just an annual appraisal—the immediate supervisor must brief his/her people on their performance in the implementation process, what they're doing right (so they'll do more of it) and what they are doing wrong (so they'll stop it). Feedback sessions between staff members and their supervisors also provide the opportunity to identify performance gaps and requirements for training and coaching.

The more aware a supervisor is of a staff person's performance and provides training and coaching, the more likely that person will take the right action toward successful implementation.

Feedback is the breakfast of champions.

Ken Blanchard

By providing feedback on the progress of the implementation continually, the organization creates closed-loop learning. Over time, it becomes a true "learning organization."

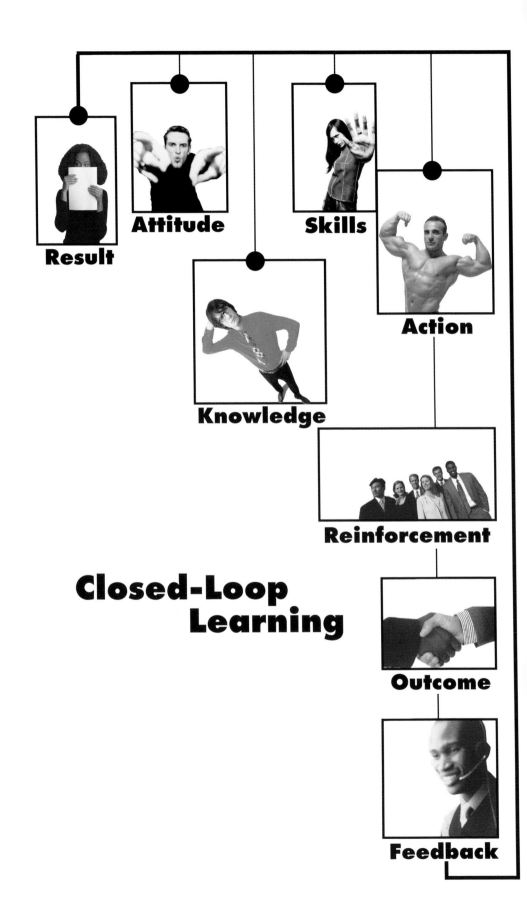

Result

Attitude

Skills

Action

Knowledge

Reinforcement

Closed-Loop
Learning

Outcome

Feedback

OROTC

(pronounced OR-OT-IC)

Remember the old expression "the devil is in the detail"? Detailed planning ensures that the right actions achieve the right results. The form of detailed planning called OROTC ensures that people in the organization take the right actions.

Specifically, OROTC is a tool that Bridges uses to assist clients not only in creating the right actions but also in making sure they happen.

The following five guidelines are summarized under the mnemonic OROTC.

OBJECTIVE

RESULT

OWNER

TIMELINE

CATEGORIZATION?

BJECTIVE

Every action must have a stated objective that defines clearly what needs to be done. The objective includes a verb that indicates action.

For example:
Objective: Interview staff members to understand their perspectives on adopting the new software.

RESULT

The right outcome for when the action is complete.

For example:
Result: Ensure the preparation work before Going Live addresses staff needs and concerns.

OWNER

The owner is the person responsible and accountable for overseeing and implementing the action—but he/she is not necessarily the person who has to take the action. Someone must take responsibility for ensuring it's completed successfully and on time, even though that person delegates doing the action to others.

For example:
Owner: Operations Manager.

Make your actions **OROTC.**

TIMELINE

Each action must have a completion date no more than three months away. But why three months?

First, if the action can't be completed within three months, then it's too large an action step. For example, "Implement the Balanced Scorecard Within 12 Months" is such a large action that it should be broken down into smaller steps.

Second, in today's rapidly changing environment, with so much to do, a task not completed within three months frequently gets delayed or may become irrelevant. A best practice is to devise a plan of action that inculcates a sense of urgency by specifying actions that will be carried out in 90 days or less.

For example:
Timeline: Complete interviews with staff members by the end of next month

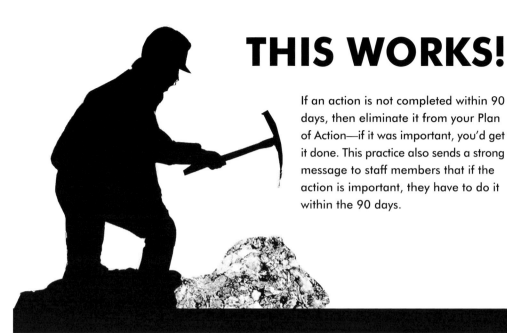

THIS WORKS!

If an action is not completed within 90 days, then eliminate it from your Plan of Action—if it was important, you'd get it done. This practice also sends a strong message to staff members that if the action is important, they have to do it within the 90 days.

ategory/Categorization?

When a plan of action is created, every item on it becomes a priority. However, leaders need clearer direction on which actions are urgent and important to the implementation. Yes, all the items are important, otherwise they wouldn't be on the list. But they need to be guided to the ones that are more urgent and important than others.

To further illustrate the timeline and allow for easier tracking during reviews, it's best to categorize actions to be completed within seven days, one month, or three months. Then further categorize them as "Must do" (important), "Should do" (urgent), or "Could do" (optional).

Following these five steps ensures that the right actions are prioritized, relevant and create an impact. It communicates to all what they need to do, why they should do it and what they should do first.

Completion
Date:
31st March

Owner
S Tan,
Marketing VP

Action: Identify a Communication Strategy

Result:
All employees
understand
the new strategy
and know why it
has been changed

Catergorization:
Must do
(within one month)

Moving Forward

1. Before taking action, get prepared.

2. Ask the three fundamental questions to help your organization identify the desired result.

3. Consider the philosophy of action.

4. Review the eight elements of right action as they apply to your organization and initiative.

5. Adopt the OROTC guidelines to make sure the individual actions are clearly stated, prioritized and deemed the right actions to take.

The following chapter looks at people and the dynamics of change—typical roles that different staff members adopt during implementation.

When you build bridges, you can keep crossing them.
Rick Pitino, basketball coach

Everything in life is mind over matter.
If you don't mind, it doesn't matter.
Satchel Paige (1906-1982), baseball pitcher

Power comes from living in the present moment,
where you can take the action to create the future.
Sanaya Roman, author

Action may not always bring happiness;
but there is no happiness without action.
Benjamin Disraeli (1804-1881), statesman

We are what we do repeatedly. Excellence is, therefore,
not an act but a habit.
Aristotle, philosopher (384-322 B.C.)

Action is the antidote to despair.
Joan Baez, singer

Thought is action in rehearsal.
Sigmund Freud, psychoanalyst

The more you overcome your reluctance and take action,
the more you realize just how often things can go well for you.
Caterina Rando, speaker and author

All the beautiful sentiments in the world weigh less
than a single lovely action.
James Russell Lowell (1819-1891), diplomat and poet

Nothing is as frightening as ignorance in action.
Johann Wolfgang von Goethe, poet and scientist

- To find your way through the implementation maze, take the right action.

- Too often, managers have no sense of priorities in their implementation activities. They need to understand which actions are critical for the future of the organization and which are mundane.

- Focus on the actions that will have the greatest impact on the right results.

- As an organization enters the maze of implementation, its leaders will find out soon enough if the strategy is working and where it needs to be altered.

- Integrate "measures" to guide you through the maze and "reviews" to give you feedback on performance.

- Everyone in the organization must say "I am responsible for the change."

- Ask: What are you contributing today to make change a reality in your organization?

- Recognize staff members who adopt the implementation early. One of the best forms comes from a person's immediate supervisor saying two simple words: thank you.

- The more aware a supervisor is of a staff person's performance and provides training and coaching, the more likely that person will take the right action toward successful implementation.

- Make your actions **OROTC.**

- If an action is not completed within 90 days, eliminate it from your plan of action—if it was important, you'd get it done. This practice also sends a strong message to staff members that if the action is important, they have to do it within the 90 days.

- Too often, leaders of organizations don't clearly visualize the destination.

- In reality, the bar of expectations frequently gets lowered along the way and anticipated results change.

- Make the strategy come alive by taking the right action and making the organization's success everyone's success.

- Beware! Some organizations become consumed with defining the destination and wait too long to take action.

- Inaction or inertia is still the enemy of progress.

References
[1]Douglas K. Smith, HYPERLINK
"http://www.bettermanagement.com"
www.bettermanagement.com, 1st April 2003
[2]Covey, Stephen R. The 7 Habits of Highly Effective People,
Simon & Schuster 1990, page 95

chapter 4
PEOPLE
We're Only Human, After All

It is not the leaders who implement the strategy but the people who do the day-to-day work—the staff. Staff members react in a variety of ways to the challenge of finding their way across the bridge. Therefore, it is important to identify and understand how they are likely to react to the new strategy and lead them accordingly.

"People Resist Change"

These three words can be responsible for the downfall of many a change process or implementation.

But they don't just resist change: they resist the unknown. They resist because they don't know how the change will affect them—how will they benefit or suffer? They want to know if supporting the implementation will help or hinder their careers. Will it be a good move to be seen as a supporter? Will their boss support this initiative? Will it take them to new opportunities?

Why People resist Change:

Fear of the Unknown
Need for Security
No Desire to Change
Security Feels Threatened
Poor Timing
Lack of Resources

This chapter demonstrates that most people in an organization either actively support an implementation or passively "go with the flowtime" once they understand its impact. Only a small minority will continually resist it.

For example, consider the transformation that email has brought about. Initially, many people resisted using it and avoided the whole Internet phenomenon. In a few short years though, email has become a part of most people's daily life. Initial resistance came because people saw learning how to use it as a challenge but its benefits as a communication tool have so far outweighed its learning challenges that it has been rapidly adopted around the world.

Organizations often fail to implement their strategies successfully because they tend to focus on the people who resist the implementation. It's now time to focus on the people who support it.

One of the main reasons organizations fail to implement their strategy successfully is because they tend to focus on the people who resist the implementation. It's time to focus on the people who support it.

Most people in an organization either actively support an implementation or passively "go with the flow", once they understand its impact.

Dynamics of Change

The term "implementing strategy" translates to staff members as their having to change the way they work and/or "more work!" They generally respond to change in one of three ways:-

➲ **Indifference**

➲ **Resistance**

➲ **Support**

Across the organization, the distribution of these three different responses falls into a bell curve (see the diagram below).

On the left side of the curve is the 20 percent of staff members who resist change. These people tend to complain about anything and everything. They badmouth the implementation process behind the leader's back and complain that the money should be spent on bonuses instead of on lost causes like yet another management fad!

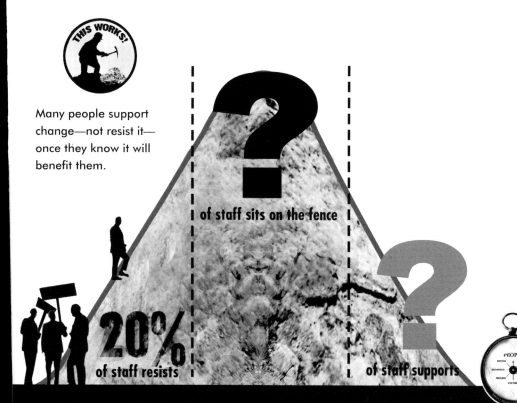

Many people support change—not resist it— once they know it will benefit them.

of staff sits on the fence

20% of staff resists

of staff supports

Dynamics Of Change

The distribution of how people respond to change

The middle group of the bell curve, comprising 60 percent of the staff, sits on the fence. These people neither support the implementation nor oppose it. They come in at 9:00 each morning and leave at 6:00 each evening. In between, they just do their work. They don't volunteer for additional work, but they don't actively resist change.

The final 20 percent are those who welcome the change, embrace it and willingly support it.

They're the early adopters and are drivers of the change.

As a leader wanting to successfully implement your new strategy, which group should you focus on? Do you start with the 20 percent who resist, believing that if you can convince them, you can convince anyone? Maybe you believe that if others see these diehards coming on board, they may go along with the strategy, too.

Perhaps you should start with the 60 percent in the middle? After all, they form the largest group. By getting them on board, you'd be building momentum, right?

Or do you start with the 20 percent who welcome the change, the ones who actually drive the implementation and make it happen?

Take a moment to think about your answer...

The right group to focus on is the 20 percent who welcome and support the change. Why?

In earlier chapters, you saw how difficult it can be to make implementation come alive. You know the odds are stacked against you, even before you start. So, make it as easy as possible for your organization to succeed. The 20 percent who support the implementation will come on board more readily than the others. **Many of them recognize the need for change without being told the reasons. They see the benefits and immediately start to take action.**

By starting here, you'll attain early wins that can be shared and celebrated with the rest of the organization. In addition, this group provides you with the feedback necessary for tweaking and improving the implementation.

While this positive group is adopting the implementation, they influence the middle group. Remember, those in the middle group sit on the fence and could fall either way. If they're influenced by the positive 20 percent however, they'll start to respond positively to the implementation. They're called the followers. Although that middle 60 percent don't charge out of the starting gate, you can move them along at a steady pace in the right direction.

Once you have 80 percent of the organization moving in the right direction, you've created a critical mass and built up enough impetus for the strategy to start. But what happens to the remaining 20 percent, those who resist the change?

About half of these (10 percent of the total staff) will resist but, if handled correctly, they will eventually start to move in the right direction. They drag their feet and make a lot of noise, but ultimately fall into line. If you're lucky, the remaining 10 percent will leave your organization and join your favorite competitor! Maybe they had the right competencies when they were hired, but today, they'll slow you down and possibly cause trouble. **Regard them as not being right for the job. It's time to say, "Thank you and goodbye!"**

General Electric uses a similar approach to this bell curve, calling it the vitality curve. The vitality curve, also in the shape of a bell curve, identifies the top 20 percent of performers, the middle 70 percent and the bottom 10 percent. Every year, the bottom 10 percent is asked to leave.

In the early years, letting that number of people go is easy, but it becomes tougher each year as fewer weak links remain. As a result, the standard gets raised higher and higher.

To help remember these groups I have given them names based on their characteristics:

Groupies—sit on the fence
Mavericks—support and
Saboteurs—resist

After a few years, I started to notice a fourth group emerge, who were initially hidden. This group is called Double Agents.

Let's now look at all the groups in more detail.

Double Agents-initially resist but can become Mavericks

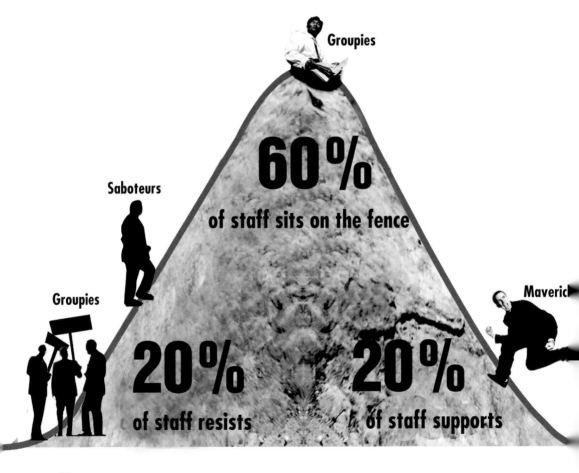

Dynamics of Change Characteristics

GROUPIES

Groupies believe there is safety in numbers. For example at 12:30 p.m., you'll see Groupies heading for lunch in groups and at 1:30 p.m., you'll see them return, still in the protection of the group. When the boss asks for a volunteer, Groupies take a step backward and stay well clear of the spotlight. Their preference is to come in, do their work and go home again. They ask few questions and do as they're told. They are often overlooked for promotions, as the following story illustrates:

A retired executive vice president at a bank was asked to return to speak to the current management team. He started by introducing himself: "I'm Mr. Tan. Many of you don't know me—I retired from this company several years ago. Since then, I've had a lot of time to reflect on my career here. I started out as a teller and eventually worked my way up to a senior management position. As I thought about those days, something bothered me. Of the hundreds of employees I supervised and managed, I can remember the names of about 20 percent whom I would classify as no good."

"I can also remember the names of about the same number who were outstanding. Together, that's 35 to 40 percent of everyone I managed. What really bothers me is that the remaining 60 t o 65 percent who came in and did their jobs every day were the most responsible for my success in the bank and I can't remember any of their names."

"I hope that when you retire, you don't bear that burden."

Groupies are the backbone of an organization. They get the job done and play a critical part in its operations.

Implementation is impossible without hundreds or thousands of people involved.

Identifying Groupies

To identify Groupies in your organization, ask:
Who is likely to be passive even though the change is an opportunity for them?
Look for those who don't volunteer but also don't actively oppose change; those who tend to go with the flow. When change is introduced, they don't respond immediately but wait for others to respond first, then they follow. This can be either an advantage or a disaster. If they follow the Mavericks, great! But if they follow the Saboteurs...

SABOTEURS

The 20 percent who actively resist the change are called Saboteurs— those who are out to sabotage the implementation. They're the easiest of the four groups to spot because they vocally and actively resist change. They make a lot of noise and often take erroneous actions. If Saboteurs had their way, the organization would never change because they'd fight for status quo. And if Saboteurs convince the Groupies to follow them, then you, as leader, will lose the support you need to initiate change.

If the Saboteurs win, the implementation collapses.

In addition, no one likes having disgruntled staff on the team. As such, Saboteurs are frequently the most talked-about group. It requires extra effort from leaders to win them over. Unfortunately, the time, energy and effort spent managing Saboteurs can absorb the initial momentum and eventually derail the whole implementation.

It's therefore no surprise that at the start of many strategy implementations, leaders focus on overcoming the resistance from Saboteurs. This can be a recipe for disaster, as the following story illustrates:

An organization had successfully piloted a new quality initiative in one of its nine plants. Based on its early success, the leaders had planned to roll out the initiative in its eight other plants. That never happened.

In a meeting that took place after scrapping the rollout, the team identified two key reasons for the failure: (1) not considering the different cultural issues at the other plants around the region, and (2) competitiveness among the personnel at the plants. The principal reason for the failure, however, was that the project team had spent too much time focusing on the plant manager in one country who actively opposed the initiative. This manager had become a constant pain in the project team's side, undermining the initiative at every turn. In regional meetings, he challenged the results from the pilot and constantly badmouthed the initiative. A potentially beneficial change was abandoned because this Saboteur "won."

The time, energy and effort spent on managing Saboteurs can absorb the initial momentum of the change initiative and derail its whole implementation.

Identifying Saboteurs

To identify Saboteurs in your organization, ask:
Who is likely to respond actively but see the change as a threat?
Saboteurs shout the loudest and are very active but for the wrong reasons. Not all Saboteurs are bad, however, for hidden among them are…Double Agents.

DOUBLE AGENTS
(the hidden group)

After observing many teams tackle the challenges of implementation, Bridges came to recognize another group who, over time, demonstrated different characteristics. They are hidden among the Saboteurs, which is why they were not initially identified.

At the start of an implementation, Double Agents demonstrate the same characteristics as the Saboteurs, but under the right circumstances, they switch to become Mavericks—and often the finest of Mavericks.

Initially, Double Agents appear to oppose the implementation. They stand back to see if this strategy is just another management fad or if it will last. When they see it is succeeding, however, they switch from opposing it to being strong supporters. Double Agents can be recognized by their secret jargon, a code fast becoming a global language. This code can be found in any company from anywhere in the world, no matter what its core business is! To crack the code, use this crib sheet:

FOTM	— **Flavor of the month, concern that this strategy will only last four weeks**
NATO	— **No action, talk only**
SSDD	— **Same shit, different day**
TINA	— **There is no alternative**
BOHICA	— **Bend over, here it comes again**
WOFTAM	— **Waste of F#@!*% time and money**

Double Agents tend to be more senior in the organization, both in position and in years and have strongly developed opinions and ideas of their own. Maybe early in their careers, they were positive-thinking Mavericks who could see the need for change but after watching too many implementation failures, they've become increasingly skeptical and cynical. They have not yet, however, switched over to the dark side. There is still hope!

When Double Agents see that the implementation is not just another short-term management fad, they will start to support it. Double Agents, however, can't be convinced by words; they can only be convinced by action. No number of presentations, coaching, meetings, emails and conference calls will move them. They have to see the strategy being imbued into the organization. "*Actions speak louder than words*" is the guiding principle for working with Double Agents, especially as their mantra seems to be…

After all is said and done, more is said than done!

Only by their own free will Double Agents cross over and become supporters—once they see the desired actions take place.

Double Agents can't be convinced by words; they can only be convinced by actions.

Identifying Double Agents

To identify Double Agents in your organization, ask:
Who is likely to respond actively and see the change as a threat, but is open to persuasion?

While Saboteurs are the easiest to identify, Double Agents are the hardest, yet it's crucial to know who they are. This is because when Double Agents switch allegiance, they go from being your toughest opponents to your strongest supporters—not just Mavericks but top Mavericks.

MAVERICKS

These people willingly and enthusiastically support the implementation. They are Mavericks in the sense of being independent thinkers who don't follow the crowd. They take the right action based on their own initiative. Mavericks mantra is: don't ask permission to do something; just do it.

Specifically, they drive the implementation in the organization. They step up to the plate as they see the need for change. They support the new strategy because they seek ways to improve and see the implementation as an opportunity. They feel positive about the change. Mavericks are the right people for the job and the right people to focus on for successful implementation.

Mavericks become role models. Through their behavior, they translate the strategy implementation into actions that everyone can understand.

Mavericks welcome new strategy implementations; they're enthusiastic and actually like to make changes. Unfortunately, many implementations fail because the organization focuses not on supporting the Mavericks but on overcoming those who resist—the Saboteurs.

Therefore, leaders need to support their Mavericks when they demonstrate the right behaviors, to recognize their achievements and encourage them to repeat desired behaviors.

Being a Maverick is a decided advantage.
The Witch Doctors, Micklethwait and Wooldridge

Mavericks will read between the lines when they first hear about the new strategy. If it makes sense to them, they'll start to implement it without waiting to be told what to do or how to do it. Aren't these the people you want in your organization?

Many implementations fail because the organization focuses on Saboteurs rather than Mavericks.

Identifying Maverick **S**

To identify Mavericks in your organization, ask:
Who is likely to respond actively to the force of change and see it as an opportunity?
Mavericks are positively oriented and optimistic by nature. They see challenges as opportunities, not problems. They see change as a way to grow and learn, and they act instinctively to make the change happen.

A secondary question you can ask to identify Mavericks is:
If your boss told you to fire 80 percent of your staff, who would you keep?

You would probably keep the 20 percent who know how to do the job and just get on with it. This 20 percent knows how to beat the flaws in the system to deliver the results. They are the top performers who just do it. These are the Mavericks.

One additional comment on Mavericks: A small group of them are sometimes either fresh out of college and/or just about to retire. Those who have just joined an organization out of college are usually gung ho. They bring with them plenty of raw energy and enthusiasm, which is great to have when launching a new strategy. They're ready to conquer the world because they've never tried it before and aren't yet battle weary. They don't yet know what they don't know!

Bridges worked with a bank that had a specific hiring strategy. Most of the tellers in their branches were young, energetic, smiling graduates. This was often the graduates' first job and they went about their work with a raw enthusiasm that was contagious. That energy created a pleasant atmosphere and a positive service experience for the customers. Plus, they didn't carry any emotional scars from previous implementations. As such, they openly and eagerly adopted the changes.

At the other end of the spectrum are those about to retire. These people can become some of your best Mavericks because, before they retire, they want to go out with a flourish rather than fade away into the sunset. They also want to pass on their accumulated knowledge and experience to the next generation. The strategy implementation provides them that platform.

In recent years, Bridges was working with a government body that was going through a major transition. Its leaders had spent time developing the strongest strategic redesign of the operations, and they were just about to start the implementation. One of the senior officers told me his concern about a group of staff members who were near retirement. Perhaps they'd be a problem and resist the change. My reaction took him by surprise when I said, "Great! They're perfect to be our Mavericks." Sure enough as we rolled out the implementation, most of the group became Mavericks.

While serving as the mayor of New York, Rudolph Giullani created a position called "senior advisor to the mayor." The advisor's principal concern was to keep initiatives moving along. The person in the role had to be able to see the big picture and was not in charge of any specific department, thus being free to co-ordinate across several agencies without fear of the usual encroachment. This person is an example of a Maverick.

Comparing Responses

Every level and department in the organization can have any or all of the four groups.
To further identify the group, look at this cluster of common characteristics.

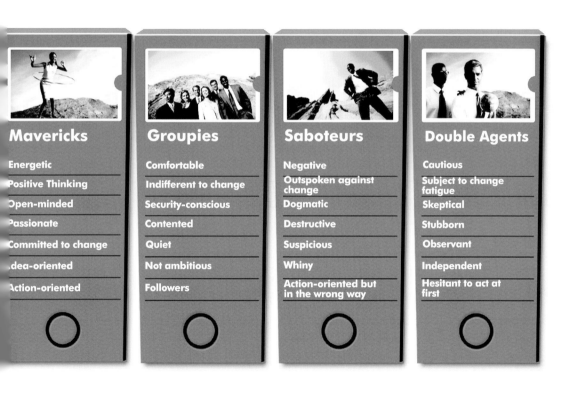

Mavericks

Energetic

Positive Thinking

Open-minded

Passionate

Committed to change

Idea-oriented

Action-oriented

Groupies

Comfortable

Indifferent to change

Security-conscious

Contented

Quiet

Not ambitious

Followers

Saboteurs

Negative

Outspoken against change

Dogmatic

Destructive

Suspicious

Whiny

Action-oriented but in the wrong way

Double Agents

Cautious

Subject to change fatigue

Skeptical

Stubborn

Observant

Independent

Hesitant to act at first

Focus on Mavericks

It's easy to understand why management focuses on Saboteurs rather than supporting Mavericks, a pattern that's hard to change.

Because Saboteurs make noise and can be disruptive, it's human nature to try to pacify them—the squeaky wheel gets the oil. In addition, most people don't like to hear vocal opposition. As a result, it's the Saboteurs rather than the Mavericks who get the attention.

Saboteurs absorb the leaders' time and often oppose every idea. We've seen this time and again and not just when implementing change. In a typical scenario, a sales manager has a team of 20 people. Their performance typically falls into the pattern of the bell curve, where 4 of them (20 percent) don't achieve their target, 12 of them (60 percent) just meet it, and the last 4 (20 percent) exceed it. But who do sales managers spend most of their time with?

Human nature dictates that they'll focus on the 20 percent who bring in less than 20 percent of the revenue! As crazy as that may sound, that's how too many sales teams in too many organizations operate.

By spending more time on the 20 percent of high achievers, sales managers could focus on where the most revenue is being generated, then share their best practices with the rest of the team. In fact, we see this tendency whenever we run the Bricks to Bridges workshop.

(For information on this workshop email: bridges@bridgesconsultancy.com.) When discussing the Dynamics of Change, most participants focus on the Saboteurs and ask how they can manage or lead this disruptive group.

Realizing that implementing strategy is tough enough, why make it even tougher by focusing your limited energy, time and resources on a group of people who want to see you fail?

Instead, focus on those who will support you, drive the change to give you early successes.

Focus on the Mavericks.

> *The only person who likes change is a wet baby.*
> *Unknown*

> *Change doesn't come from a slogan or a speech. It happens because you put the right people in place to make it happen.*
> *Jack Welch*

> *You bet on people not strategies.*
> *Larry Bossidy*

> *The wise man does not give the right answers; he poses the right questions.*
> *Claude Levi Strauss*

> *When they are falling down saying, "Gee I can't do this anymore," You've got to pick them up and say, "Yes, you can and here is why." It's getting them to dream the dream.*
> *Linda Wachner, CEO Warnaco Corporation*

> *What you expect of staff members is what they deliver.*
> *Pygmalion Effect*

> *You can dream, create, design and build the most wonderful place in the world but it takes people to make the dream a reality.*
> *Walt Disney*

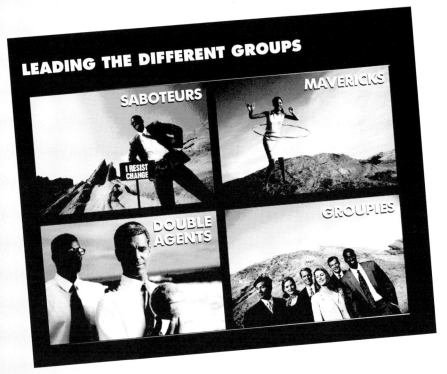

LEADING THE DIFFERENT GROUPS

SABOTEURS

MAVERICKS

DOUBLE AGENTS

GROUPIES

I RESIST CHANGE

How do you Effectively Lead each of the Groups?

Mavericks need to be **supported and rewarded** for their contributions. A leader shows the Mavericks what needs to be done and then steps back and lets them get on with it. When the results are achieved, say "thank you" and reward the people who made the implementation happen.

Groupies must be **driven and encouraged**. Groupies, remember, sit on the fence and can fall either way. Therefore it's important that a leader walks among the Groupies, driving them forward and encouraging them to get involved.

Saboteurs must be handled **carefully and effectively**. To reinforce a key message, don't let Saboteurs become the focal point of your leadership efforts.

Double Agents have to be **persuaded and convinced**. An individual, no matter how charismatic, cannot lead them. They will only come on board when they see the right actions taking effect and are convinced that the organization has crossed the point where it won't turn back.

Here's a simple, easy way to remember the effective leadership style for leading each of the different groups. This involves the three leadership styles:

1) **Lead from the front**—to lead Saboteurs through an implementation, you must be in control and hands-on. Be aware of what they are doing and how they are doing it. This means leading them from the front in the direction you want them to go rather than the direction they want to go.

2) **Lead from the middle**—with Groupies, you must get in among them. They will naturally follow, so you don't need to be at the front. But you must be among them to gently guide them in the right direction, show them what to do and encourage them along the way.

3) **Lead from behind**—with Mavericks and Double Agents, it's best to lead from behind. The Mavericks simply need to be shown what and why. Then they'll embrace the change. Your role is to support and recognize them for adopting the change and new behaviors. Double Agents cannot be pushed or challenged. Rather, they must be left to come around on their own terms with some gentle direction from behind. By communicating the actions already taken and the results achieved, they won't go amiss.

Managing Saboteurs

Despite the warning to focus on supporting Mavericks and not on handling Saboteurs, Bridges most frequently gets asked, "How do you deal with Saboteurs?" The rest of the book will focus mostly on Mavericks and Groupies. The next section addresses dealing with Saboteurs.

There is no single approach for dealing with Saboteurs, but a combination of approaches can work, depending on your situation.

One such approach is to steamroll through them by creating a strong, positive and vibrant environment that supports and rewards the staff who choose to get involved. An old cliché is *what you focus on is what you get*. Therefore, focus on the Mavericks and you create the environment for implementation—as the Saboteurs are pushed aside. This approach works well when adopted early in the implementation and Saboteurs are scattered around the organization.

One of the most popular examples of great leadership was Sir Earnest Shackleton's extraordinary death-defying 800-mile journey in an open ship. Captain and crew traversed treacherous South Pacific waters in freezing conditions that made their rescue impossible. Having failed to arrive at the South Pole, the 28-man expedition drifted on a pack of ice of the Waddell Sea for ten months. Their ship, the Endurance, had stuck in the ice and eventually crashed and sunk hundreds of miles from land. Determined to bring all his men home safely, Shackleton faced daily challenges, especially the challenge of keeping the men's morale up.

At one point, when he realized that the ice they were drifting on was cracking up, they struck out for open water, pulling with them all their supplies, equipment and three life boats. If they traversed three miles a day, they were doing well, for the going was tough.

At one point, the ship's carpenter, overcome with despair, challenged Shackleton's right of leadership, claiming that because their ship had sunk, they were no longer going to get paid and no longer under contract, according to the ship's articles. Shackleton knew if they didn't keep moving, they would die for certain. So he steamrolled the carpenter (a Saboteur). He explained that the men were under contract to the *expedition* and not the ship, and that every one of them would get paid. He also threatened the carpenter, saying if he didn't stop, he would shoot him because his complaints were endangering the life of every other man.

Shackleton's strong leadership, determination and courage saved the lives of all 27 of his men and himself. Clearly, the moral of the story was *not* to shoot the Saboteur but steamroll over them!

There is a disadvantage of this approach. If Saboteurs are entrenched in the organization, they may counter-attack and even succeed in demolishing the strategy. For example, if Saboteurs are union leaders, steamrolling (as Captain Shackleton did) may not be the right approach.

Another approach might be to convince Saboteurs either to come on board or manage their behavior, which involves sitting down with them to understand their perspective. Here are some guidelines.

When initiating a discussion with Saboteurs:
• Listen and understand their perspective about why they're opposed to the change.
  (Don't argue, just listen and understand.)

• Encourage them to further explain their views.
  (Ask probing questions if necessary; don't accept generic comments.)

• Paraphrase back what they have said to show understanding.
  (Don't repeat the same words they used.)

When persuading Saboteurs:
• State the rationale for the change and any assumptions made.

• Support your argument with hard facts and data.

• Only ask genuine questions.

If you arrive at an impasse:
• Ask what it would take for them to change their minds.

• Ask if they would be willing to be part of a change team (explained below), to share their perspective and knowledge.

• Ask them to move to being impassive about the change (be a Groupie) so you can neutralize the problem (see next section on forming winning teams).

FORMING WINNING TEAMS

Many implementations today adopt a team structure for taking actions. If this is your approach, then carefully consider the make-up of the team.

For example, a good mix for a team of 10 people is:

2 Mavericks

7 Groupies

1 Saboteur/Double Agent

The team, as well as being a structure for implementation, is a tool for engaging Groupies and ensuring their involvement and an opportunity to manage Saboteurs. The Mavericks will drive the team and often become the team leaders; the Groupies will do the daily work; the Saboteurs will create a state of reality.

When the team is planning to implement the strategy, use Saboteurs to your advantage—they will argue and in so doing, state the stumbling blocks and excuses some staff in the organization will use. This provides the team with the ability to pre-empt the barriers and have solutions or alternatives ready. It's like team members are just waiting for an excuse to come up. As soon as they hear it, they can check the list and provide the answer! Including a Saboteur on the team is a good idea, because some may be Double Agents; participating in the team becomes the catalyst for them to switch to being Mavericks.

Recognizing that people respond differently to strategy implementation and that leaders must adopt different styles for different groups, let's look at how you can present and position the strategy implementation to the staff. Consider the biz case in the following chapter.

- Most people in an organization either actively support an implementation or passively "go with the flow" once they understand its impact.

- Many people support change—not resist it—once they know it will benefit them.

- Groupies are the backbone of an organization. They get the job done and play a critical part in its operations.

- Double Agents can't be convinced by words they can only be convinced by actions.

- Mavericks become role models. Through their behavior, they translate the strategy implementation into actions that everyone can understand.

- One of the main reasons organizations fail to implement their strategy successfully is because they tend to focus on the people who resist the implementation. It's time to focus on the people who support it.

- Implementation is impossible without hundreds or thousands of people involved.

- If the Saboteurs win, the implementation collapses.

- The time, energy and effort spent on managing Saboteurs can absorb the initial momentum of the change initiative and derail its whole implementation.

- Many implementations fail because the organization focuses on Saboteurs rather than Mavericks.

This
WORKS!

Staff members need to know not only what is expected from them but also why.

chapter 5
The Biz Case
Hook, Line and Sinker

You might be asking: "Why is the organization embarking on this new journey across yet another bridge? Why should I participate in building it? What must I do?"

The answers to these questions start to make up the biz case, which hooks staff members into taking the right actions when leaders present it well. This chapter addresses how to position the benefits of the biz case to staff members and explains how they can prepare for what they must do.

Engaging Staff

Tapping into both emotions and reason, the biz case focuses on *hooking* people into the implementation. Most leaders know they must explain the benefits from the new strategy in order to encourage staff to participate. This step is generally known as WIIFM—an acronym for "What's In It For Me?" But on its own, WIIFM is not enough.

These Four Steps are Required:

- Identify the business case

- Identify "what's in it for me" (WII-FM)

- Tell staff members what's expected from them (another "radio" station, WEX-FM)

- Provide the tools and techniques—T&T—needed to succeed

  Let's look first at the biz case.

The Biz Case

The biz case clearly states the numerical and emotional rationale for adopting the strategy. It explains what will happen if the organization implements the strategy versus status quo (for example, the organization may have to close plants or lay people off or start to lose money). It also explains what will happen when the strategy is successful (for example, the organization will expand into new markets, improve productivity and customer loyalty).

A solid biz case must create a sense of urgency and drive people to take action.

When setting up the biz case, be careful to explain it from different stakeholders' perspectives. The importance of implementing the new strategy must be positioned correctly to segmented audiences: your presentation to board members, for example, will be different from the one you make to the call center team.

The people driving the strategy often become so focused and consumed with the challenge ahead that they fail to consider how others in the organization will perceive it. They don't put themselves in their colleagues' shoes or consider *why* their colleagues should stop doing what they're doing today and change the way they work. Employees are already struggling to complete what they are doing now, never mind taking on the additional work required during an implementation. After all, implementation generally means *more work for everyone!* Explaining to them *why* from *their* point of view provides the rationale and a starting point.

The biz case explains the rationale for change in the language of the audience.

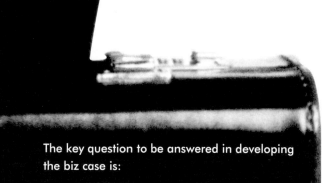

The key question to be answered in developing the biz case is:

Why is this strategy center stage?

Leaders should include three key requirements in their answer to this question:

1. Articulate the **numbers required,** both financial and non-financial (e.g., customer satisfaction rate, turn-around time and on time delivery).

2. Supply the **supporting arguments for selecting specific numbers.** Clearly state any assumptions up front. The implementation team of one organization Bridges worked with found that while it was relatively easy to state the costs savings, the proposed increase in revenue was more difficult and could be challenged. Once the assumptions made in calculating the increase in revenue were clarified, the challenges were dramatically reduced.

3. Explain the **drivers of change.** An organization may want to shift from a product-centric model to a customer-centric model because of falling customer satisfaction, low employee satisfaction and increasing costs. A snapshot of the current business climate might show good results and a stable stock price at present, but unless the organization improves its customer focus, future results will suffer.

Example of a Biz Case

Widget Co. has been losing market share because its best-selling product is becoming obsolete. Although a revolutionary product when it was launched, it's now being reverse—engineered by the competition, who are also finding ways around the patents.

Customers are losing confidence in the company's ability to design the next wave of products.

The company's "New Wave" strategy will accelerate R&D cycle time, improve the product's brand image and inject a new revenue stream into the business starting in Q3 of the company's financial year.

What's in it for Me (WII-FM)

Having established the biz case for a strategy implementation,
you must next address the WII-FM question by articulating the
benefits staff will derive from it.

When they first hear about the strategy implementation, staff
members will try to determine for themselves what the impact
will be. It is like when you see a picture of a party you attended,
the first person you look for is yourself.

It takes a determined and conscious effort to think of others before
you think of yourself and such altruism is seldom demonstrated;
the first thing each person asks is, "How will the implementation
affect me?"

Appreciating and realizing this, be prepared with the answer before
you kick off the strategy. Describe the impact of it to different parties,
show how it will benefit them as participants and explain how they
will benefit after it succeeds. People will be concerned they may
lose their jobs or their authority, so be prepared to address every
individual's concern because each one is key to making the
implementation work. Doing so spurs on their motivation to get
behind the strategy with action.

Failing to do so has been the downfall of many a strategy implementation.

Be prepared to describe the impact of
the strategy to different parties, show
how it will benefit them to participate
and explain how they will benefit after
it succeeds.

What's Expected from Me (WEX-FM)

Staff members will ask the WEX-FM question: *What am I expected to do?* It's critical that you clearly explain what they must do differently *next Monday morning* to kick start the implementation.

The WEX-FM must clearly instruct each and every individual touched by the implementation on actions to take immediately.

Think back over the launch of different strategies you've been part of but were not directly responsible for. Did anyone ever clearly explain what you needed to do differently and how you should do it? If so, how often did this happen?

Experience has shown that little or no time is spent preparing and communicating what the organization needs its people to do differently.

A leader announces the organization is going to adopt ERP, or Six Sigma, or a customer service strategy—but what do these things really mean when it comes to performing daily activities?

For example, if an ERP is being adopted, you may want staff members to support the migration of data and participate in training classes to learn the new screens. If it's Six Sigma, they can participate by becoming a Green Belt or being part of a cross-functional process redesign. If it's a customer service strategy, they can become involved by managing their individual customer touch points.

When planning the implementation, identifying what you expect people to do isn't a major challenge so don't make it complicated. From an individual's point of view, it might simply mean joining a team, meeting new customers or mapping a process.

Tools & Techniques
—T&T

You've stated the rationale in the biz case, you've explained the benefits and you've communicated what people are expected to do. The final component is to provide employees with the tools and techniques (T&T) they will need to succeed. Set them up to succeed, not fail. Beware! As sensible and simple as that may sound, organizations repeatedly get it wrong.

Don't set your staff up to fail by not providing the tools needed to succeed.

You may want staff members to use new software, map out the path of the customer, redesign a project, develop facilitation skills or gain additional knowledge. It's your responsibility to identify what tools or techniques are required, then provide the training or support to ensure they'll have the ability to succeed.

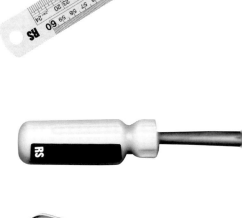

Ask: What skills and competencies do staff members need that they do not have today?

Then fill in any gaps by providing the appropriate training.

People need three things to make strategy implementation work:

- Motivation—why it is important
- Means—how it can be accomplished
- Opportunity—the chance to make it work, to do their best

Case Study 1: Citigroup and Six Sigma

In 1997, John Reed, ex-chairman and CEO of Citigroup (then Citibank), asked how Citigroup could continue to distance itself from its competitors. Citibank was number one in many of the markets but its managers fully appreciated that other banks were aiming for the top spot. So the bank had to adopt a strategy not just to stay at number one, but also to out-do the competition.

Citigroup used an excellent internal best practice to identify the strategy. It created five teams made up of its best performers and brought them to its HQ in New York.

Working in isolation from each other, the teams were asked to spend up to three months researching and creating answers to the question "How can Citigroup continue to distance itself from its competitors?" During the three months, the CEO's office helped them gain access to information and entry to other companies. At the end of three months, the teams reported their recommendations to John Reed. Several different strategies were considered; implementing Six Sigma was selected. Six Sigma is a structured approach to improving busines performance, driven by measurement and process improvement.

One of the main reasons for selecting Six Sigma was that it would involve every Citigroup person. That wasn't easy, considering there were almost 100,000 Citigroupers in 100 countries around the world. The biz case and goal of the implementation were explained to everyone and they were given the tools and techniques needed to succeed.

The Biz Case:

- **Unacceptable levels of customer satisfaction**
- **Numerous impediments to serving the customer**
- **Too many problems...too many mistakes...too long to do things**
- **Widespread employee concerns**
- **Increasing competition**

WII-FM:

Citigroup was (and still is) a demanding culture to work in, with 12 hours probably being a short day! By improving work processes, staff members finished their work earlier because they had to deal with less rework. Customers started to compliment them on their services, rather than complain about them, and many employees had the opportunity to participate in larger redesigns that challenged the basic way the bank worked.

WEX-FM:

All Citigroupers around the world knew what they were expected to do to improve their own working processes. They focused on reducing the time it took them to do their work and the number of mistakes made.

Tools and Techniques:

Every Citigrouper was trained in Six Sigma and taught *how* to map out the work.

In addition to training, reward and recognition systems were implemented and performance measurements were adjusted. Senior leaders started to track results in their business reviews. In some regions, compensation was tied to results based on the new strategy.

Case Study 2: Telco

The CEO of a prominent telephone company announced that he wanted to see customer satisfaction improve by five absolute percentage points because the competition was closing the gap on satisfaction levels. He declared that if the company could meet the CEO's customer satisfaction target, then everyone on staff would receive a bonus.

Next, he explained the business rationale and made sure staff members knew the benefits of their participation in the new strategy. But at year's end, the customer satisfaction index remained unchanged. The index failed to go up largely because the organization didn't tell staff members how to improve customer satisfaction. Its leaders never explained the main drivers of customer satisfaction and didn't describe what could be done differently to improve the customer experience. It's no surprise that nothing changed.

 In preparing to implement your new strategy, remember to clearly articulate the rationale for adopting it. Explain the benefits from each individual's perspective. Ensure everyone who's expected to participate knows what to do differently. Make sure each person has the right tools and techniques to succeed.

- Staff members need to know not only what is expected from them but also why.

- A solid biz case must create a sense of urgency and drive people to take action.

- The biz case explains the rationale for change in the language of the audience.

- Be prepared to describe the impact of the strategy to different parties, show how it will benefit them as participants and explain how they will benefit after it succeeds.

- The WEX-FM must clearly instruct each and every individual touched by the implementation on actions to take immediately.

- People need three things to make strategy implementation work:
  1. Motivation—why it is important
  2. Means—how it can be accomplished
  3. Opportunity—the chance to make it work, to do their best

- Don't set your staff up to fail by not providing the tools needed to succeed.

- In preparing to implement your new strategy, remember to clearly articulate the rationale for adopting it. Explain the benefits from each individual's perspective. Ensure everyone who's expected to participate knows what to do differently. Make sure each person has the right tools and techniques to succeed.

chapter 6

shout it from the highest mountaintop

When crossing the bridge to reach a new horizon, how do staff members know what to do and why they should do it? Their response depends on whether leaders convey the goals and necessary actions in ways that they understand.

Effective communication is not simply an email or a town hall meeting; it requires a coherent internal branding strategy. Let me explain.

An early stage in implementing strategy requires building awareness and understanding. To do this, wise leaders will climb to the top of the highest mountain and shout out the strategy to the whole organization. That's not easy!

Every year, language continues to evolve and become more complex. Just consider this progression:

When Shakespeare wrote Hamlet in 1600, he had a lexicon of 20,000 words from which to work.

When Lincoln scribbled the Gettysburg address on the back of an envelope in 1863, he had about 114,000 words at his disposal.

The Hanuoo people in New Guinea have a different name for 92 varieties of rice, which is extremely important in their economy.

Today, there are more than 600,000 words defined in Webster's Dictionary.

Language is continuously evolving...

* A mouse was a rodent
* A window was something you gazed out of
* A keyboard came attached with a piano
* A curser used profanity
* A virus was the flu
* A hard drive was a long car trip
* A web was a spider's home
* A net caught fish
* A program was a TV show
* A CD was a type of bank account
* An application was for employment
* Logging on was adding wood to the fire
* Memory was something forgotten with age

-Anonymous

In business, leaders tend to overcomplicate communication, making it hard for people to understand the simplest of messages. Your goal in communicating a new strategy should be straightforward—to enable staff members to understand what's changing; to explain why the organization is changing; and to define what they should do differently. Yet to communicate these simple messages, leaders frequently adopt ambiguous terms, blurring the strategy's objectives and goals and leaving people confused and baffled.

In business, leaders tend to overcomplicate communication, making it hard for staff members to understand their desired message.

You've heard the acronym KISS—keep it simple, stupid. It seems most organizations ignored KISS and adopted KICC—keep it confusing and complicated. It's possible people can be more confused *after* communicating about a new strategy than before the communication. It's been said that enlightenment comes out of confusion, but come on!

KISS Vs KICC

keep it simple, stupid.

Senior managers get lulled into believing that a well-conceived strategy communicated to the organization equals implementation.

Communication must be simple, engaging and easy to understand. Key messages about the new strategy should be communicated in different ways because different people have different ways of learning. (Remember the old saying, different folks, different strokes?) Also, the better the communication, the less the resistance you'll receive to the change. If people know...

• **Why the organization is changing**

• **What they need to do**

• **How they will benefit**

• **What the impact will be**

• **How long the implementation will last**

then they're more likely to support and adopt the change.

Excellent communication
equals less resistance.

Communication Strategy
coordinated, structured and consistent

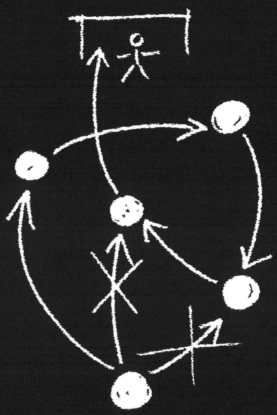

Communication is a process,
not a one-time event.

Commonly, leaders struggle to agree on *how* a message should be disseminated before they agree *what* should be said and why. They take time in meetings discussing the medium without considering the message. Should we create a website? How many pages should it have? How about making posters? What about an email from the CEO? These questions are thrown around frivolously. Often, they end up distracting the team from creating a coordinated, structured and consistent message.

It's better to focus on forming a clear and well-crafted communication strategy that guides you through the process to achieving results. Your strategy needs to start with a communication statement.

Communication Statement

An organization's communication statement reflects its communication objective. This powerful statement structures communication activities, ensuring that employees not only hear the right message but hear it in many different ways. In fact, it should be so well heard that listeners can repeat the message back in a two-way process.

Set up a team to oversee and take responsibility for creating the communication strategy. Depending on the breadth of the strategy, you could involve two people or a large group. It is, however, best to limit the number to 20; a group larger than this is unlikely to be viable.

Appoint a facilitator to guide the team through the creation of the communication strategy. This can be achieved in a one-day workshop. Here are suggested questions for the facilitator to ask.

1. What is our goal? Crystallize what we want to communicate in a one-line statement. The goal is often created after determining the communication SWOT (strengths, weaknesses, opportunities, threats) analysis. Develop objectives. What do we want to achieve and by when?

2. Who is the target audience? Who do we want to influence? Who are the target audiences? How are these audiences prioritized?

3. What is the context or environment? What has been done before and worked? What has been done before and not worked? What is the organization's culture? How does the organizational culture affect the implementation process? What are the critical success factors (CSF)?

4. What are the key messages? What messages do we need to apply to be consistent with other parts of the organization? What are the messages based on and what are possible supporting facts? What is the WII-FM? What is the WEX-FM?

5. How do we brand the communication strategy? What core theme or big idea can we develop that ties the program together in a creative, easily understood and memorable fashion?

6. Tactics and activities. What tactics and activities do we need to develop in a phased way to achieve the objectives across all target audiences?

7. Outcomes. How will we know when we have achieved our communication objectives? What quantitative and qualitative measurements do we need to show we're achieving the desired outcomes?

8. Timeline and budget. What is the timeline for the activities? What is the budget for accomplishing these activities?

Case Study

One organization preparing to roll out ERP (Enterprise Resource Planning) created the following communication strategy statement:

To move staff directly impacted by the ERP project from awareness and understanding to ownership and action, through sustained, consistent and coherent communication.

From this statement, they developed the following communication objectives:

- Develop a greater understanding of the ERP project

- Encourage country/entity management, key users and users to support the implementation of the ERP project

- Guide and manage the impact of the ERP project

- Build the common language of the ERP project

- Encourage country/entity management, key users and other users to take ownership and action of the new system after "going live".

Choosing The Right Medium

Now—and only now—are you ready to consider the different media and frequency of communication by asking: What is the preferred way of communicating an important message to staff in your organization?

This is as important as the message itself. Just as the non-verbal clues of body language influence the way a message is understood, the method an organization uses to communicate its message will influence the way it is perceived.

Town Hall Meetings, I Don't Think So

Town hall meetings involve gathering everyone (or almost everyone) in the organization into one room to hear the CEO deliver a speech introducing the new strategy. While this has the advantage of being relatively fast and easy, it's a poor mode of communication for delivering important messages. The majority of staff attending the meeting is more likely to talk about the food served or the latest gossip than the message the CEO is sharing. A town hall meeting is too impersonal and too generic.

Town hall meetings are a poor means of communicating important messages.

The town hall environment can also be intimidating. When the CEO asks for questions, most people don't want to draw attention to themselves in front of the whole organization by asking a question, even if they have one.

One client Bridges worked with was adopting a major new strategy. The team leader had spent two weeks traveling the region using a two-hour electronic presentation to explain it. The presentation consisted of more than 150 slides and introduced various new terms. After taking her *"roadshow"* around the region, the team leader was surprised that people still asked questions about topics she'd covered in the presentation. To make matters worse, she would chastise participants for asking questions. Imagine the effectiveness of that scenario. Many had trouble understanding the new strategy and those brave enough to ask were belittled in front of their colleagues.

It is important to create an environment that fosters participation and gives people the confidence to ask questions.

Town hall meetings can have solid purposes such as sharing an urgent message with everyone in the organization at once. But even then, they may be the wrong delivery mode, as the following story shows.

The CEO of an organization that was undergoing a difficult time called a town hall meeting to explain what was going on and to reassure his staff that no layoffs were planned. He thought by taking this unorthodox yet preemptive step, he would prevent panic and uncertainty. To the horror and confusion of the CEO, panic swept through the organization! You see, they had never called a town hall meeting before. The very act of calling one sent out the wrong message. It got staff members talking through the avenue that carries the most impact—the grapevine.

Email, I don't think so...

Despite the phenomenal rise and popularity of email, the medium of preference for communicating a new strategy is seldom—if ever at all—via email. Although it's an excellent form of communication for everyday use, email should rarely be used as a stand-alone means of communicating an important message.

Email is a one-way communication that may or may not be read, considering that communication is made up of:

- **7% – Alignment between your words**
- **35% – Tone of voice**
- **58% – Body language**

Therefore consider that when you send an email only 7% of the message is communicated.

A short, well-written email with a catchy title has a good chance of catching people's attention, but even then, the message must still be reinforced by a variety of other means. Different people learn in different ways. By varying the means of communication, you stand a better chance of having staff members understand the message. By constantly repeating it, you also emphasize its importance.

Okay, so if town meetings and email announcements don't work, what *does* work?

The Cascade Kit

To identify the best way to communicate, let's first look at the way people prefer to *receive* an important message.

In many organizations, staff members prefer having a small meeting with their immediate supervisor. One of the tools used to communicate a key message this way is a *cascade kit*.

The cascade kit consists of a 45-minute structured briefing. It has the benefit of delivering the message to small groups in which people can feel comfortable and ask questions. The kit contains a standard message delivered to everyone and provides a way to measure the success of the communication.

The person most listened to by staff members is their immediate supervisor.

People typically remember only about a third of what is said to them.

The cascade kit is built on the principle that the person to whom people listen most is their immediate supervisor. Using this principle, you can create a communication package to assist general managers to brief their immediate reports. They in turn will brief their immediate reports and so on, until the message has been cascaded throughout the organization and everyone has received the same information.

The typical cascade kit consists of:
- **an electronic presentation**
- **speaker notes and a video on how to conduct a briefing session**
- **a video as a secondary means of delivering the message**
- **a one-page Frequently Asked Questions (FAQ) sheet**
- **cascade feedback form**

Let's take a closer look at these elements.

Electronic Presentation

Using standard software, a supervisor presents the objectives and challenges of the strategy to a small group of his or her reports. The 45-minute slide show explains what support is being provided and highlights the key activities. The slides deliver the message using graphics and short summary points rather than text-heavy paragraphs. They are designed to be interactive and engage audiences irrespective of their cultural diversity or learning styles.

for cascade briefing is between 5 and 12 people. Groups of this size foster an environment that encourages people to participate, especially when it's their supervisor who hosts the briefing.

Speaker Notes and Session Delivery Video

The presenter is provided with notes that describe what needs to be said for each slide. This leaves him or her free to translate into the local language when required and to provide local examples for greater relevance and context. The notes indicate where the presenter can ad lib or include departmental examples. The video is an earlier recorded briefing that shows supervisors what is expected from them and provides additional training to help the supervisor deliver the core message efficiently and effectively.

Video

This video is a three to five minute summary of the key messages and is shown to the group and is another visual mode of delivery repeating and reinforcing the standard message.

FAQ Sheet

The one-page Frequently Asked Questions (FAQ) sheet makes it easy for the presenter to respond consistently to questions raised during the group discussion—again helping to ensure a uniform understanding of the strategy across the organization. At the end of the presentation, members of the group are given FAQ sheets as a take-home reminder.

Having a way to collect feedback is crucial to the effectiveness of the cascade kit. To gather feedback, the steering committee (see Chapter 10) conducts short feedback sessions with frontline staff members within three months of their receiving the kit.

The purpose of asking for feedback is to:

- ensure that everyone has been briefed personally by his/her immediate supervisor
- ensure that the cascading is completed over a short time
- identify what staff members know and don't know about the strategy
- identify what the general impact of the communication has been to date.

Other Modes

Apart from the cascade kit and the various approaches discussed above, here are some different ways you can communicate or reinforce messages within the organization:

newsletters	T-shirts	screensavers
mouse pads	caps	briefings
workshops	circulars	notice board
intranet	video conferencing	

Most organizations already use these approaches. **If, however, you really want to catch people's attention, it is best to break the pattern and adopt new, highly creative communication techniques.**

Many organizations make the mistake of frontloading the communication. They provide too much information too soon with little or no follow-up.

When a new strategy is rolled out, trumpets blow, presentations are prepared, emails are sent and videoconferences are organized. But after the initial fanfare, what actually gets communicated? In many organizations, very little. Having a long-term communication strategy ensures that staff members hear a consistent message—**and hear it consistently.**

The benefit of having a long-term communication strategy is that it ensures staff members hear a consistent message—and hear it consistently.

There is a marketing rule called 7x7, which is a shorthand way of saying, "Give people the message seven times in seven different ways." That means making sure people have heard, understood and implemented the message because you've told it to them using different modes. Different people will notice different things every time they hear the message.

An advertising maxim states that you must see a billboard six times before you will remember it.

Similarly, staff members won't adopt a strategy until they hear about it several times and remember it.

"7X7" means telling people the message seven times in seven different ways.

Clearly, sending one email isn't enough. You must also hold a meeting, print a newsletter, celebrate a hero, mention the topic at the start of every meeting for three months, create a hologram of the message, even pass out a token that symbolizes the message (e.g., if the message is about time delivery, give everyone a watch).

For important messages, your goal is to break the pattern of normal information flow across the organization and find different ways to communicate. The list below contains further suggestions for creative communications with your staff.

::Creative Communication Ideas::

Interactive web pages

CD ROM of key messages

Paper messages left on everyone's desk

Reminder signs in the lift

Fortune cookies

Laser displays at the entrance

Posters

T-shirts

Coasters

Spot Check Competition

Mad hat day

Office open day

Treasure hunt

E-newsletter

Event launch

Book about the strategy topic

Daily broadcast through email

Stationery or Post-It notes

Meetings that kick off with an opening question e.g., what have we done this week?

Share ideas during appraisal review

Question and Answer sessions

Panel discussions

Induction for new employees

Quizzes, games and competition

Video in the canteen

Car labels

Anthem

Cheerleaders

Radio shows/ TV shows (through sponsors)

Staff asked to design posters

Staff asked to design email header

Message in pay slip

Quizzes on strategy

Blank wall—employees are invited to put up suggestions for improvement, then set up a team to work on it.

Blank wall—called "voice of the customers" where guests provide immediate feedback on service and receive cards saying, "Thank you for your feedback."

Senior managers as coaches—give them each a whistle, hat and stopwatch!

"Secretary for their secretary"—have the boss use the secretary's desk for a day and play the role of secretary or check-in or reservations.

"Log book"—lists actions staff has taken to further the strategy and publish significant ones in newsletter.

Experience product by role-playing—be a customer for a day and publish customer's thoughts and feelings about their experiences in the newsletters.

Cheese and wine evening

Strategy tool kit—everything you need to make the strategy from a guide book, cards with key questions to ask, a map, a compass for direction, to a chocolate biscuit in case you get hungry or an aspirin in case it becomes too much!

An implementation bag—pencil sharpener to stay sharp, magnifying glass to stay focused, aspirin for the overtime, rubber band to stay flexible, biscuit to take a break, juggling balls to juggle all the work, mirror to keep smiling, joy stick, five senses.

Strategy video montage—different departments will be given video cameras and challenged to create a montage of staff going the extra mile in their department.

Strategy crossword puzzle.

Advice column—write in your staff problems and respond with solutions in a column: Dear Agony Aunt and Unbelievable Uncle.

Take home icon—e.g., give out watches as a reward for an on-time take-off.

Strategy hat—it gets passed around each department, each week to the person who demonstrates the behavior supporting the strategy. That person must find someone to pass it to.

Employees act as customers.

Plug & Trumpet—a plug represents plugging the source of problems to stop the bad and a trumpet represents hailing accomplishments.

Speakers Council—individuals voted on to a council that meets once a month or quarter to provide feedback on how staff members perceive the initiative.

Lunch meetings to discuss progress. (Brown Bag Lunches.)

Pulse meetings—host weekly tea or coffee with junior staff on a rotation basis plus open discussions.

Half-day staff retreat—review current state and solicit ideas.

Sessions with customers—understand their needs and help them understand our desire to create a more meaningful partnership.

Annual customer day—invite family members.

Customers are given smile cards to pass out to helpful staff members.

Activity every month—e.g., on the last Friday of the month, everyone wears the strategy t-shirt and does a strategy activity.

Visit companies who have completed a successful implementation.

Individual department launches.

Thank you cards.

Recognition day.

Charity events.

Certificates that certify people to be creative, empowered.

Company-organized debates.

113

Posters in the toilet stalls.

Fortune-telling machine.

Face painting.

Meals with names.

End of the day gift.

Start of the day gift.

Half-day booster.

Tickertape on computer screens.

Pop-up message on computer screens.

Punch bag with face.

Advertisements that including filming and interviewing customers.

Theme song.

Internal radio station.

Employee day off to do community work.

Open House for the community.

Gift basket for customers to celebrate their anniversary of doing business with you.

Work with customers on their charitable pursuits.

Bring-your-customer-to-work day.

Joint year-end party with customers.

Reward long-service employees with cool and fun equipment e.g., chair, stereo, art, toys, etc.

And my Favorites...

Have the CEO record a short
message and, over the weekend,
upload it on the phone system so
that first thing Monday morning,
everyone gets a phone message
from the CEO reinforcing the
importance of the strategy.

Controversial statement to grab
people's attention.

Storyboard—a collection of pictures
that tell a story.

Create Confusion

Sometimes you'll need to create confusion to make a strategy come alive! Make sure, however, that's it's a conscious effort to confuse them, not an unintended one.

Why would you want to create additional confusion? Well. you *can* spend increasingly more time building awareness and understanding, but it may be easier and more effective to unintentionally confuse your staff! Here's why.

> ### *If you can't convince them, confuse them.*
> *Harry Truman, former president of the United States of America*

When an organization is in a state of equilibrium, nothing changes. So, to create change, you must move from equilibrium to chaos and then back to equilibrium.

During a state of chaos, people are unsure about which path to follow through the maze. When they're in this state, they're easier to lead and less resistant because they are unsure.

By creating confusion, you will make it easier to move the organization in the direction it needs to go.

So why bother even developing a communication strategy?

Because after the organization has moved from equilibrium to chaos, it must move back to equilibrium. Yet it can only move back to equilibrium when staff members have understood, adopted and started to demonstrate elements of the new strategy. Therefore, the state of confusion is only an initial tactic to create activity. As a long-term strategy, it can lead to disaster.

When people are confused, be sure to lead them effectively—onto the right path. This requires rolling out the message (using the cascade kit or other techniques) in a way that has a single, clear focus. Also recall that Groupies (who respond passively to strategy even though change provides an opportunity for them) tend to follow those who shout loudest, whether they are Mavericks or Saboteurs. As a result, the Saboteurs might lead the Groupies astray.

Keeping It Real,
Keeping It Alive.

After you've launched the strategy and staff members have become aware of it, understood and adopted it, provide them with regular updates.

Updates will keep staff informed of progress using a variety of means, just like the initial communication. Newsletters are a popular mode, whether online or hardcopy. But you'll need more than just one means of delivering the message—not everybody reads newsletters.

Your goal is to inform people about what's happening. You want to share successes and keep the strategy alive by varying the communication mode. It's important to pay careful attention to the content of the messages. Although it might be tempting to exaggerate successes or underplay failures, honesty is the best policy.

Provide regular and accurate updates on the implementation process to all staff members.

There can be a difference between what you communicate and what the employees perceive to be really happening. That's when your strategy can lose its credibility. People quickly pick up disparities between what leaders tell them and what they see happening. Any discrepancy can be powerful enough to discourage them from participating in the strategy and can eventually derail the whole process.

Any difference between what you are communicating and what the employees perceive to be really happening can cause the strategy to lose credibility.

Communicate by using the two attention styles: emotional and numerical.

Make sure that your reported updates address people's different learning and *attention styles*. People usually rely on one of the two main styles—a fact widely exploited in advertising. The styles are emotional and numerical (which is both quantitative and qualitative).

In the initial stages, many strategy implementations make use of emotional stories to build the case for pursuing the strategy and show early successes. For example, a travel company wanted to create a higher level of customer service. They told the story about a customer who had left his passport and ticket in a bank on Friday afternoon and was scheduled to travel the next day. He called the travel company in a panic. A company representative found out the name of the branch manager, obtained his home number and arranged to collect the passport and ticket for the customer—all before his flight was due to depart and on a Saturday when the bank was closed.

This story exemplified the new behaviors that managers wanted to see from their staff.

As you roll out your organization's new strategy, start balancing stories with facts and data. Telling emotionally focused stories helps persuade people to adopt a new strategy. But stories don't work for everyone and, by themselves, they aren't enough. Many people in organizations are left-brained, which means they rely on facts and numbers to form opinions. Others are right-brained, which means they're more likely to be moved by stories and experiences than knowing just the facts.

For example, if you walk into some Chief Financial Officer's office and start to discuss the emotional side of the strategy implementation by sharing stories, you will probably get a lukewarm reception at best. If, however, you walk in and start talking about the number of new customers you have won, the cost savings and additional revenue generated, you will see his eyes open wide and will have succeeded in engaging him.

Senior managers can come to believe that a well-conceived strategy, communicated effectively to the whole organization, equals implementation. While communication is a critical component of the implementation process, it's just that—one component only. The next chapter looks at the equally important need for measuring success.

Don't be lulled into believing that a well-conceived strategy communicated to the organization equals implementation.

I forget what I hear
I remember what I see
I learn what I do.
Chinese Proverb

People don't care what you know until they know that you care.
David Lifeberman

Put it before them briefly so they will read it, clearly so they will appreciate
it, picturesquely so they will remember it
and above all accurately so they will be guided by its light.
Joseph Pulitzer (1847-1911)

Without credible communication and a lot of it, employees' hearts
and minds are never captured.
Paul Niven

If you have an important point to make, don't try to be subtle or clever.
Use a pile driver. Hit the point once. Then come back and hit it again,
then hit it a third time with a tremendous whack.
Sir Winston Churchill (1874-1965)

The greatest problem with communication is the illusion that is has
been accomplished.
George Bernard Shaw

- Excellent communication equals less resistance.

- Communication is a process, not a one-time event.

- The person most listened to by staff members is their immediate supervisor.

- The benefit of having a long-term communication strategy is that it ensures staff members hear a consistent message—and hear it consistently.

- "7x7" means giving people the message seven times in seven different ways.

- Provide regular and accurate updates on the implementation process to all staff members.

- Communicate by using the two attention styles: **emotional and numerical**

- In business, leaders tend to overcomplicate communication, making it hard for staff members to understand their desired message.

- Senior managers get lulled into believing that a well-conceived strategy communicated to the organization equals implementation.

- Town hall meetings are a poor means of communicating important messages.

- People typically remember only about a third of what is said to them.

- Many organizations make the mistake of frontloading the communication. They provide too much information too soon with little or no follow-up.

- Any difference between what you are communicating and what the staff members perceive to be actually happening can cause the strategy to lose credibility.

- Don't be lulled into believing that a well-conceived strategy communicated to the organization equals implementation.

chapter 7
Measurement
– The Guiding Light

Measurement is the light that guides the organization through the implementation maze. It tells you where it's heading and when you need to amend your course.

When you can measure what you are speaking about, and express it in numbers, you know something about it; but when you cannot measure it, when you cannot express it in numbers, your knowledge is of a meager and unsatisfactory kind.

Lord Kelvin, scientist

When transforming your organization, you deal with two measures:

strategic and operational.

Strategic Measures

In the last few years, organizations have improved their business management tremendously by using a variety of key measures that indicate the whole organization's performance. This change is partly due to the highly influential work of Robert Kaplan and David Norton, who launched their thoughts in a 1992 Harvard Business Review article called "The Balanced Scorecard—Measures that Drive Performance." A breakthrough for management performance, their ideas were rapidly picked up by many organizations around the world.

Before the introduction of the Balanced Scorecard, many organizations relied mainly on financial measures for tracking their performance. The problem, however, is that financials are lagging indicators of performance, which means they tell you the result after the business had been concluded. By that time, it's too late to influence or change the result (legitimately, that is!).

The Balanced Scorecard, on the other hand, provides a balanced perspective on the whole business, not just the financial results. It allows management to identify leading indicators and make changes that can eventually influence the financial results and overall business. The Balanced Scorecard is a tool for measuring and managing a business.

Adapting the organization's measurement system to the change agenda is critical for success.
Kaplan and Norton

Do not rely only on financial indicators. Have a balance of measures that indicate performance across the business.

Although much has been said and written about the Balanced Scorecard, we still find that it confuses many people. Following is a simplified introduction.

The Balanced Scorecard-

A Simplified Perspective

Most, if not all, organizations have financial indicators already in place: revenue growth, return on assets, operating margin, etc. The Balanced Scorecard requires the organization to develop measures in other key areas. Kaplan and Norton's research identified four areas, or quadrants, that a business needs to measure.
They are:

Financial

Customer

Process

Learning and Growth

Financial

The financials provide a powerful set of measures to judge the health of an organization. Over the years, they have become mostly standardized and globally accepted. Financial measures, however, tell you the story *after* events have happened. They tell you how well the organization has performed in serving its customers or selling its products. Because it's historical data, there's nothing you can do to change the results.

Therefore, financial results alone aren't enough because they don't allow you to change the result *and* they only provide a partial view of the business. An organization must look beyond financial indicators as a stand-alone performance measurement.

Customer

Because of the correlation between customers and revenue, an organization must measure—and act on—its customer performance. For example, the more satisfied customers are, the more likely they are to return and buy from you again. Dissatisfied customers are noticeable by their absence. How do you measure their level of satisfaction?

The Balanced Scorecard asks organizations to determine what the organization's value proposition is to its customers; that is, *why should customers buy from you rather than your competitors?* Knowing that drives the organization to put measures in place to track its performance against the stated value proposition. It's scary in today's business environment when organizations don't know if they are actually satisfying their customers or even who their segmented market is. The Balanced Scorecard puts in place the discipline to identify the organization's value proposition and segment its market. It also puts in place measures that allow the organization to understand how customers perceive the product or service and to better manage the customer relationship.

The relationship between each of the quadrants on a Balanced Scorecard is not necessarily a direct one. Increasing customer satisfaction doesn't always directly lead to increased revenue; many other factors such as interest rates, competition and politics enter into the equation.

The more satisfied customers are, the more likely they are to return and buy from you again.

Process

The Balanced Scorecard goes further by asking this question: How can we improve customer indicators *such* as customer satisfaction? One key solution is to improve processes. By reducing cycle time, reducing defects and improving productivity, for example, customers receive better products and/or services.

Improved processes can boost customer satisfaction and thus increase profits. Various quality initiatives (e.g., Total Quality Management and ISO) have focused on improving productivity to get desired results. As overall productivity improves, customer satisfaction typically improves too because customers are receiving better products or services.

The Balanced Scorecard will help the organization to identify where it needs to excel internally because it incorporates key measures to track performance.

Learning and Growth

Exactly what improves productivity? Well, the employees do the work, therefore a key way to improve productivity is to improve staff competencies through learning and growth. As staff members become more competent, productivity improves, leading to an improvement in customer satisfaction and eventually profit.

Productivity, customer satisfaction and revenue don't improve simultaneously but lag behind. In fact, it may take weeks or months before improved staff competencies result in improved profit.

Changing The Way You Do Business

Vision — **Objective** — **Plan of Action**

Strategy — **Measures** — **Results**

The Balanced Scorecard is being adopted by many organizations because it translates the strategy into action and reflects the overall performance of the organization.

The Balanced Scorecard first translates the strategy (which is aligned to the vision) into objectives in the four quadrants. Every objective then has at least one measure to track its performance. The Balanced Scorecard will drive the right actions in the organization and help bring about the right results.

The following story exemplifies the danger of an organization relying on financial measures alone and ignoring others.

The Xerox Story

In the 1970s, Xerox had a virtual monopoly on plain paper copiers. It leased rather than sold the machines to customers and earned additional revenue from every copy made. Its revenue—not only from leasing but also from supporting items such as toner—was growing steadily.

From a financial perspective, everything looked great.

Things were not quite as rosy from the customer's perspective. The machines kept breaking down and Xerox, rather than redesigning the machines to make them more reliable, saw a revenue opportunity.

They allowed customers to buy the machines directly instead of leasing, then they established an extensive field service focus as a separate profit center to repair broken machines at the customer's location.

Given the demand for its services, the division grew into a substantial contributor to Xerox's profit growth. And, as no output could come from a broken machine, customers bought back-up machines, further increasing sales revenue.

Thus all the financial indicators—sales, profit growth, ROI—were signaling a highly successful strategy. The customers, however, were unhappy; they wanted cost-effective machines.

When the Japanese introduced a more reliable copier at a more competitive price, customers left Xerox in droves.

Xerox, one of the USA's most successful companies from 1955 to 1975, almost failed. It was only by introducing a new CEO, one with a focus on quality and customers, that the company survived at all.

The Balanced Scorecard is a management tool that allows you to manage the implementation of your strategy, align the current business needs and review the whole business. For many management teams, implementing the scorecard results constitutes a complete change in the way the organization is managed.

For example, an organization might transform from financial reporting and *subjective* analysis of the results to a balanced perspective with a more *objective* and factual analysis.

To illustrate how the scorecard affects an organization's management, imagine a sales manager who justifies poor sales figures by stating that he believes customers are becoming dissatisfied with a certain company product. To support his argument, he tells a couple of emotional stories about recent meetings in which customers expressed their upset.

A shift has occurred since they started using the Balnced Scorecard. Facts and data reporting has been added to story telling. The sales manager can now report not just the financial figures but also data on declining customer saticfaction, higher defects in production and reasons for the problems.

Although the Balanced Scorecard provides a good strategic perspective, a second tier of measures at the operational level may also be required to manage the implementation process.

OPERATIONAL MEASURES

Second-tier measures at the operational level are used to gauge the impact of short-term initiatives. While the Balanced Scorecard measures the strategic perspective, operational measures show the impact of different activities at ground level.

One organization, for example, had identified its strategic position for the coming years and adopted the Balanced Scorecard to track the strategy it would implement to get there. Part of the strategy involved completing 24 different initiatives across the organization. Therefore, they had to develop operational measures for each of the initiatives to ensure they were on track.

The Balance Scorecard is used as a tool for implementing and managing strategy. Operational scorecards are used for measuring and controlling short-term projects.

Identifying operational measures for each activity is helpful for the same reasons an overall strategy needs a scorecard. These are some reasons:

- It shows the direction of the initiative.
- It shows the success of the implementation.
- It allows for corrections to be made along the way.
- It allows for measurable goals and milestones.
- It's more effective in communicating objectives.
- It's more effective for rewarding and recognizing staff.

The difference is that operational measures don't need to be balanced and they're used for a shorter period of time than strategic measures.

Learn from FedEx Example

An example of a company that uses operational measures effectively is Federal Express.

In 1990, FedEx became the first company to win the Malcolm Baldridge Quality Award for service. It has established a worldwide reputation for its operational efficiency. FedEx's secret lies in its philosophy and measurement.

FedEx believes that if you look after the people who are doing the work, they will provide good service, which will lead to improved profits. The relationship is simply this: People, Service, Profit.

Many organizations have philosophies similar to this Balanced Scorecard philosophy. FedEx is successful because its philosophy is reinforced through these measures and actions:

- an adopted service quality index (SQI, pronounced "sky")

- the company slogan ("Reach for the sky")

- mathematical measures of absolute quality failures

- compensation linked to change targets

- demonstrated values recognized through awards, e.g., Bravo Zulu (a navy signal for "job well done")

- membership in a 100% Club for those who attain 100 percent SQI for one year (includes an expense-paid four-day trip to Florida)

- Golden Falcon Award for outstanding service providers (includes 10 FedEx shares presented by Fred Smith) and 5 Star Awards (winner gets $15,000 plus stock options)

- quality is defined from the customer's perspective, not by internal standards

- daily message from the CEO, Fred Smith, broadcast worldwide at 8:30 a.m. and seen by all employees

- weighted failures to indicate relative impact on customer satisfaction

- performance tracked against 100 percent customer satisfaction and service performance goals linked to pay (SPP)

- accurate, immediate feedback of data provided to employees

- survey feedback action (SFA)

The last measure listed, SFA, enables staff members to comment on their manager's performance through surveys (see below). The manager's supervisor discusses their feedback with the manager and they agree on related action steps. If a manager under performs for an extended period, the feedback from staff can result in the manager losing his or her job.

The SFA survey asks people to rate (on a scale of 1–5) their manager's performance against the following statements: (You might want to ask your staff to answer these questions, too.)

1. My manager lets me know what is expected of me.
2. Favoritism is not a problem in my work group.
3. My manager is willing to listen to my concerns.
4. My manager lets me know when I have done a good job.
5. My manager treats me with respect and dignity.
6. My manager provides leadership and support to the quality improvement process.
7. My manager uses quality tools in my work group.
8. My manager's boss gives us the support we need.
9. Upper management pays attention to ideas and suggestions from people at my level.
10. I am proud to work for FedEx.

Customer Satisfaction begins
with Employee Satisfaction.
Fred Smith, CEO and founder of FedEx

the hierarchy of HoRRoRS

FedEx's operational measures are called the Hierarchy of Horrors—the measures having the greatest impact on customer satisfaction, which are tracked daily. FedEx also indicates the weighting of each individual measure as it impacts customer satisfaction. The measures and their weighting are shown in the table below.

Measure	Weighting
Right day, late delivery	1
Wrong day, late delivery	1
Pick-up not made	10
Lost package	10
Customer misinformed by FedEx	1
Billing and paperwork mistakes	1
Employee performance failures	1
Damaged packages	10
Complaints reopened	5

Operational Measures
in Action

Another example of operational measures comes from a sales team in a training company. The team wanted to measure the key monthly indicators of performance in four areas:

- **Product sales**
- **Proposals**
- **Revenue**
- **People**

The organization's core business, selling training programs, is based on its value proposition. It can cater to large companies of over 500 employees, and handle mass training for the whole company of 15,000 people in the region. Because of this large spread in the business, the sales team created an operational scorecard to track performance. The scorecard reflects different target markets and types of training programs sold to their clients. In addition, it tracks the team's key performance indicators such as the percentage of proposals closed, revenue and turnover.

The team's performance spreadsheet looks like this:

Measure		Result	Target
Product Sales			
No. of AB Clients vs CD Clients*		4:8	36:18
Product Mix	Product A	20%	25%
	Product B	30%	25%
	Product C	30%	30%
Proposals			
Time taken to close contract		110 days	90 days
Proposals closure		66%	90%
Revenue			
Target to date against budget		4,550,000	4,400,000
Business closed in the last 4 weeks		900,000	1,000,000
People			
Staff turnover in 12 months		0%	2%
Core competencies		58.98/90	66/90

*AB and CD are the codes given to customer segmentation

As a result of introducing the operational scorecard, there was a noticeable improvement in the team's performance. That happened because team members became clearer on what was expected of them and what they should focus on. Team leaders reviewed the operational scorecard with their direct reports. Together, they discussed and analyzed any irregularities in performance and made improvements continually.

For example, a major improvement that came from implementing an operational scorecard was adopting a competency model to review the intrinsic and extrinsic competencies of the team. Following the principle that the right people are the most important assets, the sales team created a competency model to identify each individual's strengths and areas for improvement.

In the past, the subject of generating revenues dominated their conversions. Then they shifted to reviewing individual's competencies. Benchmarking these competencies against top performers in the team created a strong, positive reaction that played a large part in the increase in performance and generated revenue.

The caliber of the people dictates the caliber of the results.

On the Implementation Compass, measures are one of the hardest to implement.

This is not because the process of creating measures is complicated, but because of the resistance from line managers as they realize their work will be regularly monitored and reviewed. The relatively straightforward process of creating measures requires a facilitator with the right experience and knowledge.

As the scorecard is being discussed (whether it is the Balanced Scorecard or an operational one), line managers become aware that their boss is going to be reviewing all aspects of their business (and in more detail) on a regular basis.

Many line managers resist the development of the scorecard because they feel threatened. Therefore, when designing a scorecard and then implementing it, leaders must be careful to define its purpose and specify how it will be used.

Measures are one of the most difficult components to implement.

Emphasize that a scorecard is not a means of control but an enabling tool for implementing strategy.

Selecting the
Right Measures...

Although the process of creating the measures is not complicated, selecting the right measures and implementing them can be challenging. This is because focusing on specific measures will affect people's behavior, as the following stories reveal:

The Call Center

A call center for an airline segments its customers and has a separate call line for its most important ones. When on a call, the line automatically disconnects after 59 minutes! Why? Because the manager of the call center gets penalized for calls lasting longer than 60 minutes.

To make it worse, key customers who had been kept waiting for almost an hour were understandably angry if or when their calls were finally answered. Knowing that, the Customer Service Officers would avoid taking these calls.

Both the measure and penalty were selected by management to ensure key customers received responsive service from the call center. In practice, however, the opposite happened.

When selecting the right measures, these managers should have first identified what's important to customers who call and then asked how they could ensure that the calls were answered well. The resulting measure is based on the customers' expectations rather then how long it takes to answer a call.

The Fast Food Chain

The outlet managers of a fast food chain paid only lip service to many of management's measures. This is because they knew the only measurement that managers rigorously checked was how much cooked chicken each outlet threw away—a measure they called "chicken efficiency."

So naturally outlet managers focused, as many people do, on keeping their bosses happy. They easily hit their chicken efficiency targets; they simply didn't cook any chicken until somebody ordered it!

If management, however, had measured a composite of indicators, they would have found that customers had to wait up to 20 minutes for their meals and had become so dissatisfied with the "fast" food service that they never returned—but at least the outlet managers hit their targets!

The Manufacturer

Managers of an automatic components manufacturer reached the company's quality measure by reclassifying as "acceptable" certain flaws that would have caused a part to be rejected in the past. In this case, the quality measure drove the wrong behavior.

The moral of all these stories is that a measure may look good on paper but it is critical to determine what behavior it will drive.

It is one thing to create and set measures and targets; it is quite another to implement them successfully. The *implementation* of a Balanced Scorecard and/or the operational scorecard requires greater diligence, attention and focus than the *creation* of the scorecard.

The next chapter addresses this question: Does your culture encourage and support the implementation of the strategy?

If you are not keeping score, then you are just practicing.
Vincent Lombardi

Shallow men believe in luck.
Strong men believe in cause and effect.
Ralph Waldo Emerson

Measure what is measurable and
make measurable what is not so.
Galileo

What you measure is what you get—what you reward is what
you get. By not aligning measurement and rewards,
you often get what you're not looking for.
Jack Welch

- Do not rely only on financial indicators. Have a balance of measures that indicate performance across the business.

- The Balance Scorecard is used as a tool for implementing and managing strategy. Operational scorecards are used for measuring and controlling short-term projects.

- Measures are one of the most difficult components to implement.

- The more satisfied customers are, the more likely they are to return and buy from you again.

- Emphasize that a scorecard is not a means of control but an enabling tool for implementing strategy.

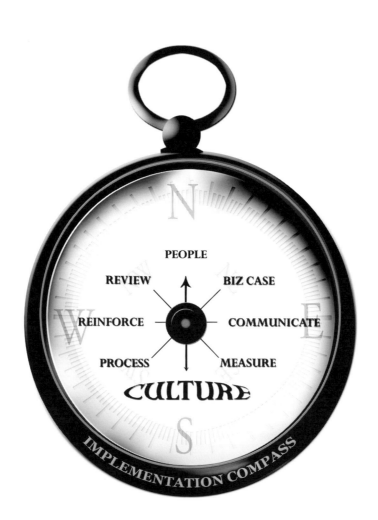

chapter 8

Organizational
Alignment Our Way or the Highway

When leaders start to build the new bridge, they convey why it is important for staff members to follow them across it and announce the measures that will guide their steps. The leaders, however, often do nothing to change the day-to-day way business is conducted. As a result, the implementation loses momentum and eventually dies.

The next two chapters address this challenge and introduce the "Cultural Life Cycle."

To align people in your organization with the strategy implementation, change their day-to-day activities.

Successful strategy implementation comes from changing the way you operate—both in the way you conduct business and the way things get done internally. To achieve this, start to change the day-to-day activities of your staff.

There's actually nothing new or startling about this instruction, but how often do managers expect to change organizational culture without changing their approach?

It is like taking a wrong turn—and then doing it again! Ludicrous? You'd be surprised just how often organizations repeat mistakes they've made before.

Organizations often expect different results from doing the same thing!

The organization's culture must support and reinforce the new strategy.

Aligning an Organization's Culture

Culture has many different meanings. In the context of strategy implementation, we define culture as **"the way that people do things in organizations."**

Culture drives the way people deal with customers, how they do their work and how they deal with problems. It drives human behavior. Culture is, in fact, what makes HP different from Dell, Citigroup different from JP Morgan and Southwest Airlines different from American Airlines.

After all, computer companies all offer technology solutions, banks all deal with money and airlines fly people from place to place. Their cultures, however, define how they do what they do differently.

Differing cultures also drive the behavior of the staff so an organization should be conscious of the culture it cultivates.

Southwest Airlines and Citigroup are two companies with very distinct cultures that drive very different behaviors from their staff.

Case Study—Southwest Airlines

Southwest Airlines is an American regional airline and one of the few, in addition to Singapore Airlines, that has continuously made a profit over the last 25 years despite wars, recessions and terrorism. Its culture of "love" and making flying fun gets reinforced throughout the organization by the way it conducts its everyday activities.

Here are some examples:

- **Its hiring process—interviews are more like acting auditions and customers sit in on the interviews;**
- **Its dress code—not jackets and ties but shorts and T-shirts**
- **Its in-flight activities led by attendants to entertain passengers—e.g., competitions to find the passengers with the biggest holes in their socks, or pranks to see how many people can fit into an aircraft toilet!**

Other legendary Southwest activities include attendants dressing up as Dracula on Halloween, and hiding in the overhead compartment to surprise the passengers when they stow their luggage. Imagine the passenger opening the overhead compartment and someone shouting from inside it, "Welcome on board!"

These activities contribute to defining Southwest Airlines' culture and drive the way its people behave. Because they're having fun, their customers do, too. When passengers get on a Southwest flight, they start to relax and enjoy themselves—the opposite of what people tend to experience on most short-haul flights.

147

Case Study—Citigroup

In the banking world, Citigroup takes the responsibility of handling customers' money very seriously. Three adjectives that describe Citigroup's culture are aggressive, ambitious and arrogant. Located in more than 100 countries around the world, Citigroup has corporate, consumer and private banking businesses. Each business competes aggressively to make deals and win market share.

Citigroup has a critical measure called "the share of wallet"—that is, how much money in the customer's wallet does Citigroup control? (Similarly, Coca-Cola measures "share of throat"—how much of what a person drinks is made by Coca-Cola?) Citigroup's internal fierce and highly competitive culture is not for the faint-hearted. The company is known for hiring already successful, top-quality, highly driven professionals and then continuing to enhance their ability.

Staff turnover is a common problem in most companies. Citigroup is no exception, especially in its treasury business. A trader typically spends a year learning the business and another year performing on the trading floor before leaving—usually to work for the competition. Competitors eagerly seek to lure them away with lucrative offers because they've been well trained at Citigroup.

The work pressure in Citigroup is intense: One mistake and you can be out. On the other hand, Citigroup recognizes good performance. For example, a trader who has an exceptional year can receive a 500 percent salary bonus!

Citigroup's arrogance is reflected through its advertising phrases such as: "When you look at the earth from the moon, 70 per cent of it is blue and some of that is water!" (Citigroup's corporate color is blue). Citigroup's edge in its industry partly comes from fostering a culture that attracts the best people and then supports and encourages them to excel.

Staff members in companies mostly do what other people do—that is, they assimilate into the culture of an organization and don't stand out. Therefore, if you want them to change the way they work to support the new strategy implementation, you will need to make sure the organization's cultural changes keep abreast of the implementation.

The organization's culture must foster and support change as demonstrated by this model of how organizations change—the culture life cycle.

Similar to the product life cycle developed by marketers that is sometimes referred to as the S-curve, the organization's culture life cycle explains why an organization must keep changing.

Let's first look at the product life.

Product Life Cycle

Every commercial product has a distinct life cycle usually in three phases, as shown in the diagram below.

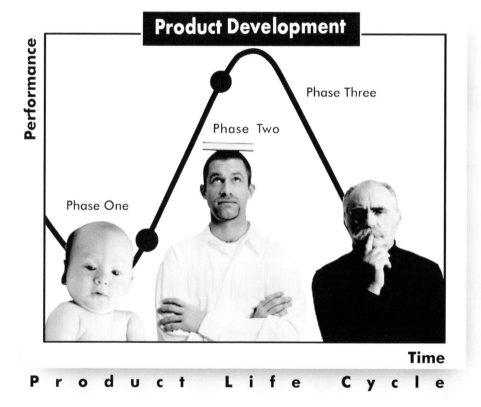

Product Development

Performance

Phase One

Phase Two

Phase Three

Time

P r o d u c t   L i f e   C y c l e

The product life cycle begins in Phase One, the birth of the product. New products typically have defects that need to be fixed and time is required to build awareness among its target audience, thus causing an initial dip in performance during this phase. In Phase Two, the product is selling well and everything looks good. In Phase Three, the product's performance has started to decline; its useful life is just about over.

The period of the life cycle varies for different products and implementation, but in general life cycles are getting shorter. Not too long ago, a car manufacturer could expect a new car to have a life cycle of 15 years; today, it's three to five years. During the height of the dotcom boom, the life cycle of software products was a mere three months; by the time it reached the shelf in the computer store, the software was already obsolete.

Organizations have to decide when they should introduce a new product (or strategy.) Andy Grove, in his book *Only the Paranoid Survive*[1], calls the moment that a new product should be introduced the "inflection point." He defines this as the point at which the old strategic picture dissolves and gives way to the new, allowing the business to ascend to new heights.

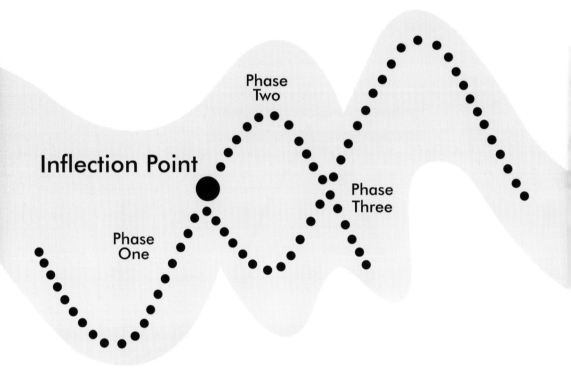

Inflection Point

Phase Two

Phase Three

Phase One

The inflection point is when the CEO starts to transform the culture of the organization.

At the inflection point, the organization should introduce its new product to the market. Likewise, it is at the inflection point that the CEO who is about to implement the strategy must ensure the culture fosters and supports the implementation.

If the organization does not foster and support it, then it is in danger of moving into Phase Three and becoming extinct.

A Culture's Life Cycle

An organization's culture follows this life cycle pattern in the same way as its products. In Phase One of the culture life cycle, the organization is just starting out. Its goals are to create cash flow and build a market for its products or services. This phase is known as the "entrepreneurial phase" in which the organization searches for the success model that will move it to Phase Two. Performance can dip as it struggles and attempts to find its base.

In Phase One, the culture tolerates mistakes since no one knows yet what works and what doesn't. Also in Phase One, the HR manager and/or CEO wants to hire people who are self-starting, self-driven and entrepreneurial. They want Mavericks.

Leaders recognize that the organization has entered Phase Two when business indicators start to improve dramatically. These indicators include increases in:

Sales
Customer Acquisition
Customer Satisfaction
Employee Satisfaction
Productivity
Market Share

In Phase Two, the organization has found its success model and puts in place the structure, systems and standards to replicate the success.

In Phase Two, if you make a mistake, your boss reprimands you because the organization has developed a set way of doing things and a standard to follow.

In Phase Two, the HR manager hires people who follow instructions and will copy the model of success. They want to hire Groupies.

An organization recognizes it has entered **Phase Three** when it sees the indicators from Phase Two start to decline. It seems obvious; you are losing business so it is time to change. Leaders, however, can miss the inflection point because they may be tracking the wrong indicators or thinking it is only a short-term slump or because they are so absorbed in daily operations that they are not looking at the business strategically. The stakes, however, are high; if the organization misses the inflection point, it may go into crisis and its very survival could be threatened.

There is, however, a paradox to this.

Culture Life Cycle Paradox

Here's the paradox of the organizational life cycle: When you are nearing the inflection point, everything is going well. That is a clear signal that it is in Phase Two and has only one direction to go—down! It is also an indicator that it is time to change. In other words, just as everything is working the way you want it to and your achieving the results, yep—it's time to change!

Leslie Wexner, CEO of The Limited Inc, elegantly states that "Success doesn't beget success. Success begets failure because the more that you know a thing works, the less likely you are to think that it won't work. When you have had a long string of victories, it's harder to see your vulnerabilities." The leader's role in the organization is to identify the inflection point in Phase Two and identify where the organization needs to change. This may mean it's time to introduce a new product, a new technology or a new strategy.

It is easier for leaders to prepare for change before reaching the inflection point than afterward.

Leaders earn their pay by being able to stand back from day-to-day operations and perceive where the organization is in its life cycle. They carefully watch for the inflection points and have the next wave of products or strategies ready to go.

It's easier for leaders to prepare for change before the organization reaches the inflection point than after it does. Once the point has passed, people might panic as they see the organization struggle to recapture falling revenue and market share as well as customer defections. As U.S. President John F. Kennedy once said, "The time to repair the roof is when the sun is shining."

Similarly, the time to change is not when indicators are sliding and problems are mounting. Make changes when you have the time, resources and revenue. But, of course, this isn't easy to do.

Imagine how people feel when the team just starts to reap the rewards for all its hard work and the CEO announces it's time to change. No wonder they resist change and think the CEO is crazy! But change they must and it's the leader's role to facilitate this necessary change process.

Understanding the consequences of not changing, the leader puts forth a business case to explain the reasons for the change. One technique is to examine what will happen if people continue along the current path and contrast this with what will happen if they do change direction.

Much like leading a group through a maze, the leader sets out on a path and requires everyone in the organization to follow it. Along the way, wrong turns and mistakes will be made but the leader must stay true to the vision of the strategy, guiding people through the mistakes and dead ends that might occur and motivating them along the way.

Breaking the pattern of success, however, in Phase Two isn't easy. There are three critical times it must be done.

Three Critical Times

Organizations create inflection points at three critical times:

Crisis—the whole organization is forced to change reactively (for example, when a competitor's new product is becoming more successful than yours)

Adoption—leadership is forced to adopt a change simply to stay in business (for example, when new technology such as the Internet is developed)

Anticipation—strategically, the leadership recognizes that the market will soon change and prepares accordingly

The most desirable of the three is anticipation because it's proactive rather than reactive. For example, Andy Grove was CEO of Intel in 1986 at a time when the company began switching from making memory chips to microprocessors. The company abandoned memory altogether and worked both to dominate the microprocessor business and turn it into a brand, as evidenced by its "Intel® Inside" campaign. Mr. Grove anticipated market demand and made the change.

An Organization that Gets It...

Over the years, Microsoft has successfully embraced the product life cycle concept.

In 1995, it introduced the operating system, Windows 95. Windows 95 had a life span of about five years but before it became obsolete, the company introduced Windows 98. This version boosted sales again—but while customers were enjoying the benefits of the new, more reliable operating system, Microsoft was already working on the next line of products. Introduced two years later, these products included Windows NT and Windows ME. In 2002, Microsoft introduced its latest operating system, Windows XP.

Microsoft is already working on its next operating system, which will be called Longhorn. This is how they stay ahead of the market: Microsoft recognizes the inflection point for its products and makes sure it has the next one ready before the existing model becomes dated.

There are normally exceptions to every rule and one product has defied the life cycle model—Coca-Cola. This soft drink has been around for over 120 years and hasn't changed. In fact, when the company tried to change it a few years ago, its customers worldwide rejected New Coke and demanded the return of Classic Coke.

The Both/and Approach

As you know, an organization does not implement strategy overnight. During the necessary transition period, old habits are forgotten and new habits adopted.

Also during the transition, staff members are asked to perform additional work. In most organizations, they're already working a full day and struggling to complete the work they already have, never mind adopting more. This gives rise to the commonly heard complaint:

"I can't find the time!"

Staff members, especially Groupies, are willing to adopt the change but finding the time to do so can be difficult.

To implement a new strategy successfully, however, it's essential for everyone to adopt the new way of doing things while still working in the old way.

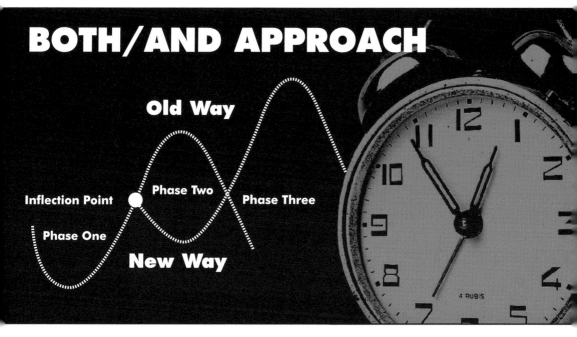

BOTH/AND APPROACH

Old Way

Inflection Point — Phase Two — Phase Three

Phase One

New Way

This period of overlap when staff work with both old and new processes is called the both/and approach. It shows up in many facets of the business. For example, instead of either investing or cutting costs, a both/and approach calls for both investment and cost-cutting.

The both/and approach appears in many different guises, such as:
* low cost and high quality
* both quantum and incremental redesign of processes
* both creative and analytical approaches
* focus on both short-term and long-term results

Failure to consider the both/and approach can be detrimental, as one sales manager discovered the hard way in this example:

A sales manager in a manufacturing company asked his team to achieve an aggressive sales goal in the 4th quarter so they could end the year on a high note. Team members responded positively and worked extremely hard over the quarter, partly inspired by the manager's promise of a lucrative Christmas bonus. The manager was delighted when the team met its targets but celebrations were cut short by the finance manager who reported that, while revenue was up, margins were down, so the sales team would be receiving a smaller bonus than the previous year, not a larger one.

The team members felt devastated. After all their hard work in the last quarter, they were being punished, not rewarded! Some even quit after receiving the bonus, blaming the failure of the company to keep its promises as the reason for leaving.

What went wrong? The higher revenue targets were met only through an aggressive advertising campaign that had successfully expanded the market and brought in new customers—but its cost had exceeded the increased revenue and thus reduced the profit margin.

This sales manager learned the lesson of the both/and approach the hard way. He now asks his team to improve the margin to ensure he gets the right results.

He also changed the bonus criteria, tying it to increased margins rather than increased sales.

Mavericks, Groupies, Saboteurs and Double Agents

In Chapter 4, we discussed the four ways different people respond to change. Nowhere are these differences clearer than in their responses to the organization's cultural life cycle.

Mavericks in the organization immediately understand the need for change and embrace it. They readily change behavior, switching paths at the inflection point (as shown in the diagram).

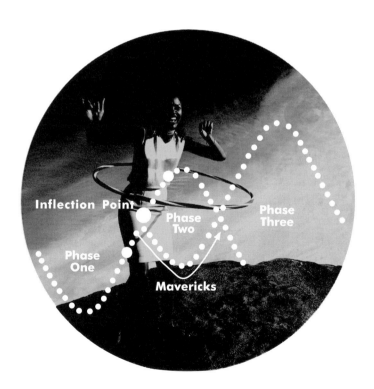

Inflection Point • Phase One • Phase Two • Phase Three • Mavericks

MAVERICKS READILY ADOPT THE NEW WAY OF DOING THINGS

Groupies tend to be undecided and try to balance the old way with the new. The path they follow depends on how the well the organization applies the disciplines of transformation.

GROUPIES ARE INDIFFERENT TO THE CHANGE AND ARE EASILY PERSUADED ONE WAY OR THE OTHER.

Saboteurs resist the whole idea of change and will stay on the old path. If the Saboteurs "win" the organization will eventually move into Phase Three and oblivion.

SABOTEURS RESIST CHANGE AND WANT STATUS QUO.

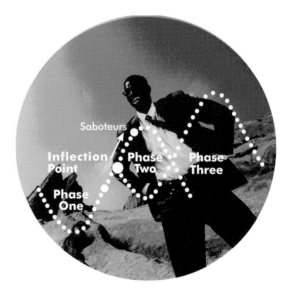

Double Agents wait to see if the organization is serious about implementing the new strategy, making sure it's not another fad or flavor of the month. They will switch over to being a Maverick when the organization stops working the old way and fully adopts the new way, if not before. The inflection point is when a new strategy should be introduced. When the organization fully commits itself and stops working the old way it is at the convergence point.

DOUBLE AGENTS WHO HAVE SEEN IT ALL BEFORE ARE WAITING TO SEE WHAT HAPPENS BEYOND THE SPEECHES AND PRESENTATIONS.

Convergence Point

As its name suggests, the convergence point is when the organization has committed itself to **the new strategy** (and/or the old product is no longer being sold). At this point, people will no longer fall back into the old way of doing things. The organization has moved from making promises about the future to actually living the future, from talking about action to implementing it. The new strategy being imbued into the organization's culture is on its way to becoming part of its DNA.

At this point, Double Agents have become convinced. **Actions, not words,** sway them to become some of your most adamant supporters—your best Mavericks. Some Double Agents may come on board earlier than this but most will wait until the convergence point.

The period between the inflection point and the convergence point is a critical stage. This is when the inflection point gets recognized and strategy implementation starts. During this time, the organization must continue to take the right actions so it will reach the convergence point.

Most strategy implementations fail between these two points. That's why it's essential to pay strict attention to detail at this stage.

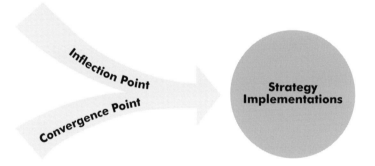

Most implementations fail between the inflection point and the convergence point.

Keep the transformation period between the inflection point and the convergence point as short as possible.

It can take anywhere from a few months to a few years to reach the convergence point from the inflection point, but it's better to strive to reach it sooner rather than later. This takes the organization from equilibrium to chaos and back again as quickly as possible.

The True Picture

The unfortunate picture of strategy implementation for most organizations looks like the diagram below.

The True Picture of 90 percent of strategy implementations

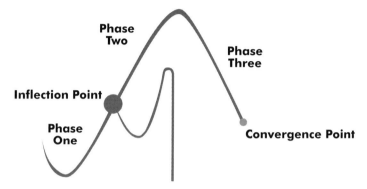

After the initial fanfare and launch of the new strategy, about 90 percent of all organizations do not achieve the desired results and all the promises and dreams fade away.

Staff members who supported the new strategy wonder why they bothered becoming involved when they see the organization's way of working go back to how it had been before—the one difference being that leaders will now have an even harder time introducing any new strategy because the staff has grown more cynical about the leadership's sincerity and ability.

And it can get Worse—

Once a strategy has failed to deliver on the leader's promise, people make a mental note about the experience and tuck it away. The more they hear and see similar broken promises, the more resistant they become.

What happens? The Groupies who were sitting on the fence fall on the side of the Saboteurs. Then, with the number of Saboteurs is equal to the number of Groupies, the leadership team faces an uphill battle to implement any kind of change. It's a fair bet that once an organization has reached this extreme state, it could already be on the slippery road to declaring bankruptcy.

It is not the strongest species that survive, nor the most intelligent, but the ones most responsive to change.

Charles Darwin

When the organization's leaders simply latch onto the latest and greatest idea (often referred to as "management by fad"), the situation keeps deteriorating. Such organizations launch the next strategy before the last one has had a chance to work (or fail), thus creating a state of perpetual change with one strategy backing up behind the last (see below).

No one knows what works and what does not and employees don't know what they should be doing. Unfortunately, this is a true picture for many organizations.

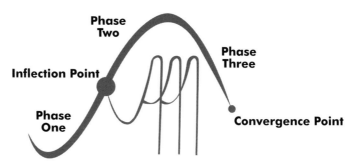

In summary, an understanding of the organization's cultural life cycle will help explain why organizations must keep adopting and implementing new strategies—or face extinction. It reinforces the message that the time to change is at the inflection point and that the strategy starts to become part of the organization's DNA at the convergence point.

Be sure to pay attention to the life cycle of your organization's culture as you implement your strategy.

- To align people in your organization with the strategy implementation, change their day-to-day activities.

- The organization's culture must support and reinforce the new strategy.

- The inflection point is when the CEO starts to transform the culture of the organization.

- It is easier for leaders to prepare for change before reaching the inflection point than afterwards.

- Keep the transformation period between the inflection point and the convergence point as short as possible.

- Organizations often expect different results from doing the same thing!

- Most implementations fail between the inflection point and the convergence point.

References

[1] Grove, Andrew S., *Only the Paranoid Survive: How to Exploit the Crisis Points That Challenge Every Company*, Doubleday, 1999, p. 32

chapter 9
Changing People's
Behavior -
no easy task!

Building bridges to your new strategy requires changing individuals' behaviors.

Looking further into the "culture" element of implementation, this chapter addresses what it takes to change how staff members behave.

Values and Environment

Defining culture as "the way we do things in an organization," it was noted that changing staff behavior is critical for the implementation. But just how do leaders change (or at least influence) the behaviors of individuals? There are two main schools of thought on this:

- Change their attitudes and values, or
- Change the environment around them

Following the "both/and approach" noted in the last chapter, there might be a third school of thought: Change both the attitude and the environment!

Changing Values

A critical part of implementation is to change staff behavior to create different results.

As a leader, you want people in your organization to work differently and achieve a change in organizational performance.

The first school of thought says that in order to change people's behaviors, you must change their fundamental values— and this is easier said than done.

Behavioral psychology shows a relationship between values, attitude and behavior. By changing people's behaviors, you can start to influence results. Values dictate attitude, which dictates behavior, which impacts organizational performance.

 Values dictate attitude, which dictates behavior, which impacts organizational performance.

If an organization is customer-focused, this value will dictate the desired behavior toward customers. For example, if you are about to leave the office at the end of the day and the phone rings, do you pick it up or continue on the way out the door?

If you value the customer, then you will answer the call. As a result, the customer receives responsive service. When these types of customer-focused actions are widespread and sustained, customer satisfaction starts to rise, as shown in the diagram below.

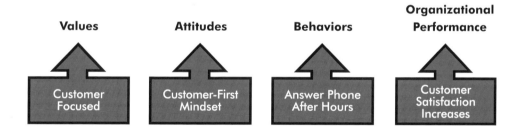

Values	Attitudes	Behaviors	Organizational Performance
Customer Focused	Customer-First Mindset	Answer Phone After Hours	Customer Satisfaction Increases

Over the last few years, many organizations have defined their core values and are seeing how those values shape their culture. So how can an organization that wants to make changes influence behaviors by changing values?

Values are part of an organization's core ideology and can be defined as **the fundamental beliefs that guide action**. As we have seen with strategies, it is easier to create values than it is to implement them. To implement values successfully, an organization must change its basic DNA. (For some organizations, it would be easier to climb Mount Everest.)

To change behavior, leaders are required to translate an intrinsic value into an extrinsic behavior. For example, integrity is a value people have within them; it's intrinsic. The leaders strive to translate that integrity into expected behaviors, which are extrinsic, e.g., delivering on promises and commitments made in meetings. In another example, telling the truth is an intrinsic value that transfers to being truthful with customers. One group of support staff Bridges worked with identified initiative as a core value and further explained the value by describing three extrinsic behaviors that demonstrated the value in action.

1. **Identifying needs**
2. **Examining relevance of processes and**
3. **Resolving problems.**

Extrinsic behaviors can be taught and encouraged through recognition and rewards. Leaders will also be able to quantify and qualify the impact of the values, encouraging the change they want to see in the behavior of their staff members. Once a value has been articulated as a behavior, it can now be seen and as such, can be measured (and managed), as the Values Inculcation Model (VIM) below indicates:

STRUCTURE FOR USING VALUES TO INFLUENCE CHANGE

VALUES INCULCATION MODEL (VIM)

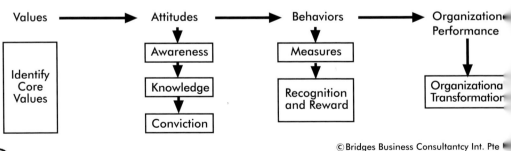

Values ⟶ Attitudes ⟶ Behaviors ⟶ Organization Performance

| Identify Core Values | Awareness | Measures | Organizational Transformation |

Attitudes: Awareness → Knowledge → Conviction

Behaviors: Measures → Recognition and Reward

Organization Performance → Organizational Transformation

©Bridges Business Consultantcy Int. Pte

VALUES INCULCATION MODEL (VIM)

The first step is to identify (or revisit) current values. There should only be four to six values; any more than that and they're no longer core values.

Defining core values isn't something organizations do on a regular basis, although more and more leaders understand the important role values play in organizational performance.

Values:

- define the areas in which the organization will not compromise—e.g., despite crises or recession or high turnover, the organization stands fast by its values

- are positively chosen and will be firmly held to—people only subscribe to those values they personally believe in, which is why top-performing organizations hire people whose values match their own

- can be clearly communicated—everyone in the organization must understand the values and therefore they must be capable of being communicated

- are internal—but their management is purely external and requires constant vigilance

- are demonstrated through the behaviors they encourage—the behavior must be managed

- are where staff members compare intentions against performance—the values state what an organization believes and staff members watch to see if they are verified through everyday actions

Once the importance of values is understood, the next step is to articulate the desired attitudes.

Before people can demonstrate the behaviors, they must adopt the right attitude by gaining the awareness, knowledge and conviction of the values.

STEP TWO: ATTITUDE

Communicating values alone will only develop awareness and knowledge, but will not generally result in a change in behavior.

Changing attitudes starts with awareness because if you are not aware of something, then you can't start to adopt it. Awareness alone, however, still isn't enough. The awareness must be fed with knowledge such as:

- Why the values are important
- Why were they selected
- What behaviors must change
- What will be their impact on the business result

After awareness and knowledge, individuals gain conviction through rational thought and encouragement from their peers. Once they've gained conviction, they'll start to change their behaviors.

STEP THREE: BEHAVIORS

Once employees have demonstrated the new behaviors, they should be encouraged to repeat them until they become the accepted way the organization performs—part of the organization's cultural DNA.

To reinforce the right behaviors, the organization's leaders then put in place measures to track performance. The measures provide feedback on the results of adopting the new behaviors and may lead to taking corrective action along the way. The information is shared with staff members so they understand how their efforts are contributing to business improvements. After measuring the impact of the new behaviors, people need to be encouraged to adopt the new desired behaviors permanently. Leaders must find ways of encouraging people to demonstrate the desired behaviors, clear any roadblocks and recognize desirable staff behaviors appropriately. Recognition can be as simple as a pat on the back and a verbal "thank you", or it can be linked to performance management (discussed in Chapter 12).

Provide staff members with positive reinforcement through rewards and recognition to encourage new behaviors.

Once leaders identify the core values as well as the attitudes and desired behaviors of staff, they can review the impact of these changes on organizational performance.

STEP FOUR: ORGANIZATIONAL PERFORMANCE

By identifying core values, changing attitudes and encouraging new behaviors, the organization will start to transform. Your role as leader is now to ensure that the culture fosters and supports the transformation and that Mavericks (the early adopters) and Groupies (the followers) are given the right support and are taking the right actions to achieve the right results.

Make sure you give ongoing attention to the actions taken and their results to ensure you're headed down the right path of the maze.

Too many leaders take their eyes off the implementation, thinking their job is done.

Many organizations struggle to implement their values. Identifying them and hanging them on the entrance wall is a common global practice. Changing the attitudes and behaviors of staff and achieving a higher level of organizational performance as a result of inculcating the values is a rare trait shared by the select few organizations considered the best in the world. Many organizations stop at just identifying values (and make a half-hearted attempt at inculcating them). The Values Inculcation Model ensures that the values directly translate to improved performance.

Changing the Environment

A critical part of implementation is to change people's behaviors in order to create different results.

This can be achieved by changing the environment around your employees.

An experiment conducted in the 1970s[1] identified the impact of the environment on behavior. A group of volunteers leading "regular" lives were placed in a simulated prison environment, while another group was selected to be their guards.

The results of this experiment were shocking and disturbing. The mock situation immediately affected the behavior of those in both groups. The guards who had volunteered became hard, demanding disciplinarians and the prisoner volunteers rebelled violently against the guards. Five prisoners had to be released due to their extreme emotional states.

Placing volunteers in a simulated environment severely altered their behaviors.

In organizations, if you want to create a fundamental change in people's behaviors, you must create an environment around them in which the desired behaviors are nurtured and encouraged.

By changing the environment, you can clearly start to change the culture—which is sometimes easier to change than the people themselves.

THIS WORKS!

It is sometimes easier to change the environment than to change the person.

Consider a time when you changed your behavior to assimilate into a new environment—perhaps when you were changing jobs. When people start new jobs, they frequently adjust their behavior to blend into the new environment. No one asks them to change their behaviors and no one promises a reward, yet they change anyway. Why? So they won't stand out. They change in order to conform and to assimilate into the new environment.

Another example is found among students studying overseas. Many students from Asia study at universities in Australia, Canada, the United States or Europe. These countries typically have a different culture from the students' home cultures so the students, who typically want to blend into their new environment, change their behavior.

If implementation requires employees to change their behavior, you can often achieve this by changing the environment.

You can start by asking these three questions:

1. **What is the change you want to see?**
2. **What new behaviors do you want staff members to demonstrate?**
3. **What will encourage them to demonstrate these behaviors?**

A large oil company wanted to change its culture and have its staff become more customer-friendly. Specifically, leaders wanted them to improve how they managed customer relationships, customer enquiries and requests. To support a cultural shift, the layout of the office was changed from high partitions and individual offices to an open space plan. The old layout had discouraged staff from talking to each other and some found it intimidating. The new layout encouraged people to talk to each other, thus creating a friendlier environment. Staff members quickly changed their behavior because of the change in their environment, an improvement immediately noticed by their customers.

Studies have shown that the simple addition of a few plants to the office helps people become more relaxed and productive. One organization even invited its employees to come in during the weekend and decorate the office however they wanted it and after that, leaders noticed an improvement in performance. Some organizations have removed all chairs from meeting rooms so, by changing the physical environment, they changed people's behavior. Meetings became shorter and more concise because people didn't want to stand around too long.

Case Study

When I first moved to
Singapore, the training consultancy I worked for,
the Service Quality Centre, took changing the environment to heart.
Because the training center was located in the north part of Singapore in an out-of-
the-way area, trainees were brought to the center by bus. As they arrived, they were
escorted off the bus into a hall where music was playing and breakfast was provided.
The environment was carefully controlled to create a positive impression and a friendly
welcome. They were given nametags so that they could easily identify each other. The
rustic surroundings immediately relaxed participants.

After being grouped into their classes, they were escorted to the training block that was
an old, colonial bungalow. Sessions were taught in the open air beside the building and
participants sat on benches. The training was dedicated to changing people's mindsets
and making them more customer-centric, therefore the hard benches intentionally made
participants feel uncomfortable and thus more receptive to the learning!

In addition, the space had no comfortable hotel-style chairs, no large conference tables,
and no air conditioning, which is common for most buildings in Singapore, where the
temperature is about 86°F every day. All of this was carefully designed for a reason:
people are more receptive to learning when they are taken out of their comfort zone.
The environment contributed to taking people out of their comfort zone and breaking
down the resistance to learning.

The course included an overnight component and no opportunity was lost to break down
the resistance to learning with participants sleeping in a dorm with five or six others.
The environment used in this seven-day course created the right results.

How Language Affects the Environment

Language usage also impacts the environment and as such, individuals' behavior. Change the language and you can change behavior.

Walt Disney understood this when he created Disneyland. The people working at Disneyland are called cast members, not employees and the personnel department is called the casting department. Uniforms are called costumes. When working with customers, cast members are "on stage." The language used by Disney contributes toward creating the Disney magic loved by children (and adults) around the world.

How does the way language is used in your organization communicate to your staff?

Language reflects the culture. Change the language and you change behavior.

Walking the Talk

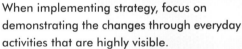

Controlling the environment to change behaviors is practiced in many organizations. When implementing strategy, people need to see changes in the social fabric of the organization and in the way that everyday activities are conducted. It's important to start with activities that are highly visible, such as:

- Departmental meetings
- Business reviews
- Conference calls
- Emails
- Corporate image
- CEO briefing
- Newsletters
- Appraisals

The challenge is to reinforce the strategy implementation through everyday activities that influence the environment.

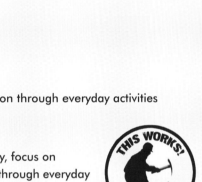

When implementing strategy, focus on demonstrating the changes through everyday activities that are highly visible.

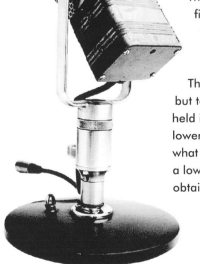

Recently, I gave keynote speeches to two different organizations. The first client was a bank that was reducing costs to meet the fierce downturn in the market. Leaders decided to go ahead with an important event, because it was a major milestone in the bank's journey and an important celebration.

This event would normally have been held at downtown hotel, but to keep in line with the company's global cost reduction, it was held in the local cinema across the road from the bank at a much lower fee. Instead of renting equipment, staff members brought in what they needed for the event and set it up themselves. They served a low-cost fast-food breakfast and a bottle of Singapore New Water, obtained free as a government promotion.

Shortly after that speech, I gave another talk to employees of a jewelry company that was celebrating service milestones. This event started with an expensive breakfast in a private room in a downtown hotel. After breakfast, attendees were escorted next door where the room was set up with a stage, lights, speakers and the equipment for the event. It featured a master of ceremonies and formal introductions.

How did the message sent to the staff differ at these two different events? Significantly.

 Staff members must see changes in the way everyday activities are conducted for organizational messages to be meaningful.

In deciding whether to focus on changing behavior by changing values and attitude or by changing the environment, or both, remember this: Every organization has to find its own path through the maze. As leaders, take time to identify what aspects will have the highest impact on encouraging people to achieve the right results.

- Values dictate attitude, which dictates behavior, which impacts organizational performance.

- Provide staff members with positive reinforcement through rewards and recognition to encourage new behaviors.

- It is sometimes easier to change the environment than to change the person.

- Language reflects the culture: Change the language and you change behavior.

- When implementing strategy, focus on demonstrating the changes through everyday activities that are highly visible.

- Staff members must see changes in the way everyday activities are conducted for organizational messages to be meaningful.

- Communicating values alone will only develop awareness and knowledge, but will not generally result in a change in behavior.

- Too many leaders take their eyes off the implementation, thinking their job is done.

References

[1] "Interpersonal Dynamics in a Simulated Prison," International Journal of Criminology and Penology, 1973, no 1 pg 73

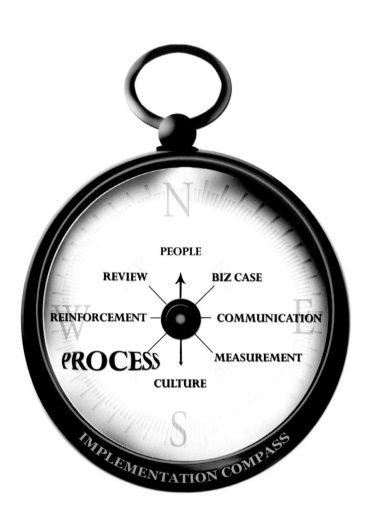

chapter 10
Process ~
Tweak, Adjust, Improve, but Align those Processes

The Implementation Compass tells you what actions to take day to day to build your bridge. The key question is, "How do you align these actions with each other to be effective?"

In this chapter, we look at what it takes to align the processes that help your organization move forward efficiently and effectively and examine the best practices you can adopt from Six Sigma.

Process alignment can be defined as:

Congruence between what you say you are going to do (strategy implementation) and what you are doing (the process).

A lousy process will consume ten times as many hours as the work itself requires. A good process will eliminate the wasted time.

Bill Gates, Business @ the Speed of Thought

Implementing strategy means reviewing the current processes and aligning them toward the new anticipated results.

Far too often, we hear these immortal words "it's time to change" and yet, after all the fanfare, the organization continues to work in the same way.

Implementing strategy means reviewing current processes and aligning them toward the new desired results. That requires you to step back from day-to-day operations, reflect on what you're doing and ask:

1. Do our current processes support the implementation?
2. How can we work more efficiently and effectively?

These two questions should be considered together, as the following example indicates.

Passengers who wanted to use the Bagnall-to-Greenfields bus line serving the Midlands area of the UK found themselves standing helplessly at bus stops as empty buses roared past them. Bus line officials had a simple explanation for this: "It's impossible for drivers to keep to their timetables if they must stop for passengers!"

A key reason why organizations fail to implement strategy successfully is because they don't change their basic ways of operating.

Over the years, leaders have seen various methods adopted for improving processes, including ISO, Crosby and Total Quality Management (TQM), to name but a few. Each method has its advantages and disadvantages.

Six Sigma has adopted the best practices of many previous methods and has gained appeal globally because of the desirable results it has produced.

If you are looking to improve your current processes as part of your strategy then instead of reinventing the wheel, consider adopting the best practices from Six Sigma. I'm not suggesting you implement Six Sigma but rather take on its best practices as a way to align your processes to your strategy implementation.

Defining 6 Sigma

Because various definitions of Six Sigma exist, you may be confused about what it is. Consider these:

- A line manager defines Six Sigma as *an all-encompassing organizational initiative that produces business disciplines and quantum leaps in results.*

- A statistician might simply define it as *managing variation.*

- The founders of Six Sigma at Motorola define it as *a measure of "goodness"—measuring the capability of a process to produce perfect work. That indicates the degree to which a product or service can be processed without creating mistakes.*

In a nutshell, Six Sigma is a structured approach to **improving business performance driven mostly by measurement and process improvement.** (That wasn't so bad, was it?)

Today, you can adopt many of the best practices from Six Sigma without having to chase the Six Sigma authorization. At Bridges, we call this the "Son of Six Sigma" because it picks the main techniques of Six Sigma and implements them where they fit.

The following best practices from Six Sigma are recommended:

1. **Link to the P&L**
2. **Structured process for improvement**
3. **Measurement system and use of absolute numbers**
4. **Quantum versus incremental process changes**
5. **Combination of hard and soft sides**
6. **Emphasis on the customer—end to end**
7. **Supporting infrastructure**

Best Practices
from Six Sigma

American-based Motorola developed Six Sigma in the 1980s in response to threats from Japanese manufacturers. In the 1960s, Japanese products were considered cheap, unreliable and poorly made. But 20 years later, products made in Japan had earned the reputation of being reliable and of high quality.

Motorola developed the Six Sigma model to improve the quality of its products. It was able to improve its profits mainly by reducing production cycle times and the number of defects. For example, it successfully slashed the production time of pagers (remember them?) from 40 hours to one hour, resulting in fewer defects, higher productivity and lower costs.

While Motorola was the company that created Six Sigma, it was General Electric (GE) who popularized it. In the late 1990s, GE was revered as the pinnacle of American business success—the organization against which other companies set their benchmarks. When GE successfully integrated Six Sigma into its business, others copied its lead and Six Sigma became a globally accepted initiative. Motorola took more than seven years to develop and implement Six Sigma but GE took only five because its leaders learned from Motorola's experience.

Don't reinvent the wheel when you can learn and adopt best practices from others who have gone before you.

If you tell your CFO that cycle times and defects have been dramatically reduced, you can expect no more than a courteous nod. But if you say you've just added $25 million to the bottom line, the CFO's eyes will open wide. You've gained that person's full attention.

One school of thought says that TQM failed on many occasions because it didn't show strong enough financial benefits. Six Sigma *demands* that expected financial benefits are stated upfront and that measures are instilled to track both financial and non-financial (e.g., cycle time and defects) results.

To calculate the financial benefits from *any* process redesign, you need to ask:

- *What is the current revenue generated from the process?—This will provide baseline data that shows where you currently are.*

- *What is the estimated financial impact of the project?—Consider both the cost savings and the potential revenue.*

- *What is the market potential?—Consider the larger picture.*

When answering these three questions, also state any assumptions you make, such as the competition not introducing a new product, interest rates staying the same or customer demands surging.

BEST PRACTICE #1

State upfront the expected financial benefits from a process improvement and instill measures to track both financial and non-financial results.

Poor processes in an organization negatively affect customers in the long run, i.e., it's the customer who ultimately suffers. Therefore, it's critical to address processes that are not adding value to the customer or the business.

Six Sigma provides a customer-focused model known as DMAIC (pronounced dee–ma–ic) for guiding an organization through process improvement and redesign. DMAIC is an acronym for:

Define opportunities—what is important?
Measure performance—how are we doing?
Analyze opportunity—what is wrong?
Improve performance—what needs to be done?
Control performance—how do we guarantee results?

Poor processes in an organization negatively affect customers in the long run.

When using this five-step process, start by identifying *what* is critical to the customer and *which* processes affect performance the most. Then gather relevant information and empirical data to identify where you are and what needs to be improved on—all based on fact and data, not hearsay. Next, systematically seek the information and knowledge you need to take action, then map and redesign the process to improve interactions experienced by the customers, the suppliers and the business.
Finally, spell out a disciplined management of the end-to-end customer experience.

Here's an example. When Bridges worked with an international bank, the leaders were deciding if a process should be migrated to an overseas central hub or remain in the country. Although the bank never embarked on Six Sigma, it did apply some of its best practices—the DMAIC model. It provided the framework to identify both the benefits and measures for the migration and helped managers understand potential cost savings, process improvements, automation and customer benefits.

The most intense step is step four of DMAIC, improving performance. This involves cross-functional process mapping (CFPM). Its name describes what it does; that is, it brings together key members from each function of a process (the term *function* is used instead of *department* because one department may have more than one function) to map a specific process.

This cross-functional team identifies issues, defines the start and stop points of the process and captures baseline data. The team then redesigns the process and tracks and measures improvements against the baseline.

CFPM benefits the organization by breaking down management silos. In a typical organization, each departmental manager is mostly concerned with his or her own silo and tends to view the whole business vertically, like this:

Sales	Marketing	Operations	Finance	HR	Legal	Distribution

CFPM aims to break down this silo thinking. It takes a key person—usually a Maverick—from each function and puts that person part-time on a team for an average of three months to map out and improve processes. During this time, the team reviews existing processes and then develops a new process to take the organization where it wants to go. As part of breaking down silo thinking, Mavericks representing different functions get to know each other and can easily seek assistance from another function later in the implementation. It also builds important group dynamics.

Here's the revised diagram:

Now, they can see the whole process from start to finish.

To ensure the right corrective action is taken based on the root cause during process redesign, the team's facilitator must keep asking "why?" Here's an example of how using the question "why?" can lead to appropriate solutions.

The Lincoln Memorial deteriorates more than the other monuments.

Why? It is cleaned more often.

Why? It has more bird droppings.

Why? There are more birds, especially sparrows, around the Lincoln Memorial than any other memorial.

Why? There are more spider mites, a sparrow's favorite food.

Why? The lighting attracts the spider mites.

What solution emerged from this questioning process? To change the lighting around the monument.

Not all process redesigns require a cross-functional team. When the process is small and can be changed through discussion rather than mapping, you can start it with these four simple questions:

1. Wouldn't it be nice if...
2. Don't do it today...but would this proposed change dramatically improve the process and make it better for the customer?
3. If we were the competition, what would we do to knock ourselves out of business?
4. What would you change if you had a magic wand or were CEO for the day?

BEST PRACTICE #2
Use a structured approach e.g., DMAIC, for making process improvements.

3 Measurement Systems — and Use of Absolute Numbers

How would you react if your son came home and said he got 93.31 percent in his exams? You would most likely be delighted (or you might ask if he cheated!). Percentages, however, can be misleading. When you convert them into absolute numbers, the figures tell a different story; 93.31% is three sigma, which translates to 66,810.63 defects per million opportunities. Suddenly you have 66,810.63 opportunities to improve a process. If a manager is told that the performance was 93%, he or she will probably not say very much. If the same manager is told that there were 66,810.63 defects, you will see a very different reaction. In a nutshell, this is why you should use absolute numbers and not percentages—it creates a stronger reaction. In addition specific and accurate measurement is critical for improving the process.

Six Sigma is a goal and without going into a complicated calculation, it translates to 3.4 defects per million opportunities. That means for every million items, all but 3.4 are produced within the defined standard. So for every million credit card transactions processed, for example, fewer than four errors occur. "Hang on" you might be saying, "we don't do anywhere near a million transactions or products." That's okay, you do not need to. In the Six Sigma calculation you multiply by a million to magnify the problem and thus create *defects per million opportunities*.

Aircraft safety is one process that continually operates above Six Sigma standards. For every million flights there are fewer than four accidents. Tracking aircraft luggage, however, operates at around three sigma, which translates to around 70,000 defects per million opportunities. This means for every 1,000 bags handled, 70 get lost.

Not every process operates at Six Sigma, or needs to, as it is sometimes neither cost effective nor required.

Airline safety operates at close to seven sigma and when there is a crash, a major investigation is conducted to identify the root cause, eliminate the problem and improve the process. For airline luggage, however, the financial and time investment in improving the process is not worth the return. In other words, it is less expensive and easier for the airlines to apologize for losing your luggage than improve and maintain a Six Sigma process.

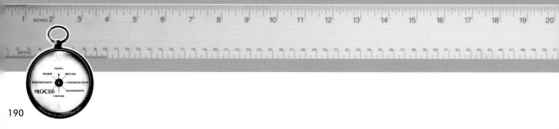

Not every process must or should
be operating at Six Sigma.

Six Sigma drives the organization to a high level of performance by magnifying the performance, which is measured in absolute numbers. It also provides the structure to identify the root cause of that performance and how to resolve it—DMAIC model.

When creating measures for your
implementation, carefully consider whether
percentages will produce the true picture.

 BEST PRACTICE #3
Every project must have clear measures and targets for success, using absolute numbers, not ratios or percentages.

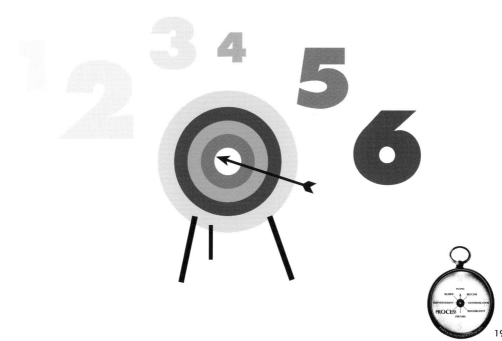

④ Quantum versus Incremental Process Changes

I'll never forget the first time I heard a presentation on re-engineering. The speaker announced that it cost a typical corporation three or four million U.S. dollars to re-engineer its organization. Yet 75 percent of re-engineering initiatives fail! Why would organizations invest millions of dollars on an initiative when the odds are stacked against its success from the start? They'd be better off gambling their money in the casino!

Clearly, changing an organization overnight is a major undertaking—a quantum leap that carries with it a high risk factor of failure.

To reduce the risk, Six Sigma takes lessons learned from re-engineered organizations. The Six Sigma model employs a project approach that combines both quantum and incremental change. It sets in motion small changes and large changes at the same time, knowing that some projects will return as much as a million dollars while others will barely cover the hurdle rate.

✔ **BEST PRACTICE #4**
Combine both quantum and incremental process improvements.

5 Combination of Hard and Soft Side

Many different initiatives over the years have failed to grasp the importance of balancing the soft and hard aspects of a business—the emotions and the numbers, the people and the processes.

Process redesign is about changing the way we work. To change a process, you must change what the people do.

Successful process redesign involves a balance between addressing the process and the people, as this diagram indicates.

Accomplishing that balance means:

- taking time to explain why the process is being changed
  (i.e., presenting the business/case)
- taking time to tell people what will change and how they will benefit
  (i.e., WII-FM—What's In It For Me)
- explaining to people what you expect them to do differently in the new process
  (i.e., WEX-FM—What's Expected From Me)
- providing the tools and training to set up the staff for success

Believe it or not, many organizations fail to take these steps. They redesign the process and then tell everyone to just do it! No communication, no explanation, no training.

Organizations can fail to provide people with the training and tools to assist them when changing processes—and then experience disastrous results.

Redesigning a process is the easier part; just like a new strategy, it is easier to create than implement.

To implement a process redesign, the redesign team takes an average of three months to map out the current process and redesign it. The redesign involves a few Mavericks led by a dedicated facilitator (in Six Sigma language, a Black or Green Belt) and is usually facilitated from a comfortable hotel meeting room where everyone is well cared for.

The team then has the challenge to implement the redesign. Its members must sell the rationale for the change to those affected. To do so, they must influence people over whom they may have no direct authority. And they must do all this while continuing to do their regular work!

The redesign implementation will take twice as long as the process design and requires that the team now move from reviewing the process (the hard side) to engaging the people impacted by the redesign (the soft side) in changing.

By not preparing for the soft side of implementation, you set yourself up for failure—and the team's future, too.

The scope of the redesign will dictate the degree of challenge facing the implementation team. Some smaller redesigns are easier and simpler to implement because they affect current operations less and involve only a few people. The larger the scope of the redesign, the more time the redesign team must dedicate to preparing for its implementation.

The larger the scope of the redesign, the more time the redesign team must dedicate to preparing for the implementation.

In preparing to implement the redesign the first four action steps needed are:

1. Develop a project plan and system to manage the implementation of the redesign process through action item teams.

2. Develop and execute a plan to communicate:
- the project status
- the steps needed to implement the redesign process
- the composition and purpose of action item teams to the stakeholders—sponsors, steering committee, team members, supervisors, facilitators and the organization at large

3. Develop and implement a system to:
- identify key performance indicators of the redesign process
- measure and report key performance indicators, e.g., defects, customer satisfaction index and cost savings, on a monthly basis (at a minimum)

4. Work with the financial controllers to:
- estimate the financial benefits of implementation associated with the action item and the project
- define actual benefits once the implementation is completed
- update the database with the financial impact each quarter (at a minimum)

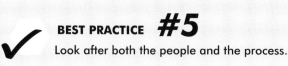

✓ **BEST PRACTICE #5**
Look after both the people and the process.

⑥ Emphasis on the Customer
—End to End

Every process starts and ends with the customer. The customer is defined as anyone who needs your services, which means the customer can be either external or internal—including colleagues, peers, managers and even your boss.

Every CFPM (cross-functional process map) requires listing all the functions touched by the process. On every list, the first person is the customer and the last person is—yep, you got it—the customer. That means when preparing to redesign the process, you must get to know your customers better than ever. Specifically, make sure you know:

- **Why they do business with you**
- **What they need from you**
- **What they expect from you**
- **What irritates them about doing business with you**
- **What would delight them**

By emphasizing customers, the result of your redesign process will be much more responsive to their needs, not just at the beginning and end but from end to end (E2E).

Every process must have the customer at its center and every step must directly or indirectly add value to the customer.

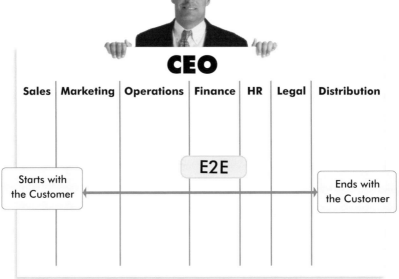

When redesigning the process,
the customer is at the center of all decisions.

When focusing E2E on customer needs, you might discover that as much as one-third of the process adds no value to the customer. This happens because some steps that have been added to the process over the years become obsolete and no longer add value to the customer or the business. For example one organization identified when it stopped to review the process for approving spending above $250,000 that 27 signatures of approval were required! Over the years more names had been added.

By mapping the process E2E, you review every step using these two questions:

1. Why do we do this?
2. Does it add value to the customer or business?

The cost savings alone can return on average U.S. $250,000 in a multi-national company. To illustrate how process steps can become obsolete, consider the following example.

For many years, the U.S. Army had a policy of waiting eight seconds between pointing its cannons at a target and actually firing them. As part of a drive to improve work processes, the army hired an external consultant. He noted this peculiar pause and queried the process. The soldiers responsible for firing the cannons told the consultant they were just following the instructions in the manual, so the consultant checked with the officers about the procedure of waiting eight seconds before firing. The officers responded that this had always been the policy. Not one to give in, the consultant searched army archives for the reason behind the eight-second wait. He discovered that the policy was a well-established tradition stretching back to the 18th century. And the reason for it? To give the soldiers time to move the horses away!

Voice of the Customer

To ensure the process is customer-centric, it's critical for the redesign team to know and understand customers' needs and expectations. Specifically, the team must understand the voice of the customer—an expression used to describe the customers' views and expectations.

 Many organizations do not solicit customer feedback or track customer satisfaction!

Many people associate customer research with a survey. But Six Sigma isn't about surveys—**it's about creating numerous listening posts to instill the voice of the customer into every part of the business.**

 It's critical to identify customer feedback proactively and not simply rely on customer comments.

When redesigning a process, the team aims to exceed customer expectations after the redesign. To do so, members must know what customers want. It's critical to identify customer feedback proactively and not to simply rely on customer comments. Various researchers have concluded that solicited feedback accounts for only five percent of an organization's total feedback; the challenge is capturing the other 95 percent—the unsolicited feedback.

How can you identify the voice of the customer?
The chart that follows offers several ideas.

Tool	Description
Focus groups	Small groups of customers invited (with a facilitator) to answer open-ended questions
Interviews	One-on-one interviews, typically held at the client's location
Formalized complaint system	A system for tracking customer complaints, providing a record for making improvements
Market research	Typically conducted by a third party to provide feedback on the market situation
Mystery shopper programs	A popular tool in the hospitality and retail industries in which unidentified individuals provide feedback on the quality of the service they receive in specific areas
Customer scorecards	A recent addition in which you measure your customers' performance as a scorecard, similar to an internal operational scorecard
Customer panels	Invite a small number of customers on a regular basis to answer open-ended questions
Data warehousing & data mining	Analyze electronically captured data for below-the-surface trends and customer profiling
Customer hotlines	Listening posts that enable customers to contact the company easily and receive a response
Complaints and compliments	Unsolicited feedback from customers
Loyalty programs	Reward and encourage repeat customer business

On occasion, leaders assume they know what customers want rather than gather empirical evidence.

Don't assume you know what customers want, rather than gather empirical evidence and also use your intuition.

Remember, conducting customer research doesn't need to be expensive. Once a week, the sales team can ask customers one question. Or the customer service officer can ask customers to fill in a questionnaire at the end of their meeting. You can also learn from the following example shows.

One of New York's leading cultural institutions was about to undertake a costly study to find out which of its many exhibits was the most popular with visitors. It invited eight different research companies to bid for the contract. Over a period of four months, decision-makers finally identified the research company they wanted to hire. However, due to the size of the investment, the contract had to be approved by the management team. Just before it was signed, somebody questioned why the organization was even hiring a research company. With everyone puzzled and curious, one of the managers suggested they look internally first to see if someone already had the information. That someone was the janitor; he told them which part of the gallery he had to mop the most. That answered the question!

Finally, a word of caution: When an organization starts to become more customer-driven and looks to identify the voice of the customer, there should be a swell of activity as each department and/or redesign team approaches its customers. Unfortunately, the team members often all approach the same person in the organization. For example, different departments in a bank all approach the CFO. In an IT organization they all approach the CIO and in a production organization they all approach the Production Manager. Therefore when starting out on internalizing the voice of the customer, make sure that the customer research is coordinated and well managed.

When you start internalizing the voice of the customer, there may be over-enthusiasm in different departments to approach the same customer. As a result, the customer is inundated with the requests for the same information.

BEST PRACTICE #6
Process redesign starts with the customer and ends with the customer.

7 Supporting/Infrastructure

Another best practice from Six Sigma is to make sure your organization's infrastructure supports the process redesign, thus giving it every opportunity to succeed.

Good project management requires identifying the following five components:

1. A project champion
2. The corporate steering committee
3. A project facilitator
4. A team leader
5. The redesign team

1 Project Champion

The project champion is one of the first positions to be filled. Commonly, this role is taken on by a senior manager with a vested interest in seeing the process redesign succeed. This person champions the cause both verbally and through action. He or she joins the corporate steering committee.

The project champion is responsible for overseeing not only the redesign of the process but also its implementation. That person's responsibility ends when the redesigned process delivers the desired results. Unfortunately, many redesign team members think they've completed their work as soon as the redesign is complete.

In reality, the work is just beginning; the redesign is only one-third of the total work while implementing it is the other two-thirds.

For the organization's first project redesign, the champion is normally the CEO or regional manager. Naming a person at such a high level signals to everyone how important management regards the initiative while it provides top-down support for the team—which may be critical.

Here's how one project champion stepped in. The redesign team of an organization came across a policy that was obsolete but still part of the process. When it created a roadblock, the team wanted to abolish it, but this corporate policy was a sacred cow and not easy to change. So in the monthly review with the project champion (the regional head), the team presented its rationale for abolishing the policy and the project champion made the abolition a priority on his personal action list. He had the policy abolished within a few days and cleared the roadblock.

 The project champion is responsible for overseeing not only the redesign of the process but also its implementation.

2 Corporate Steering Committee

Some senior managers in the organization will join the corporate steering committee, which is responsible for guiding and empowering the redesign team. The committee doesn't approve or reject the redesign, but it empowers and trusts the redesign team to do its work while providing support and assistance. Let me say that again…managers are conditioned to sitting in meetings and either approving or rejecting decisions. This is not their role in the steering committee—their role is to coach and guide the redesign team.

If the committee has to block any part of the redesign (for example, something clashes with the corporate strategy), then they must fully explain the reasons.
The steering committee's role is to:

- Ensure alignment with corporate strategy
- Remove roadblocks
- Communicate the changes
- Attend redesign team meetings
- Be accessible
- Encourage and empower others
- Support the internal marketing
- Lead by example

Project Facilitator 3

The *project facilitator,* who guides and facilitates the team through the whole project, must be trained in the competencies required for the job. In Six Sigma, facilitators are known as Black Belts or Green Belts, depending on their level of training. The project facilitator should be a competent facilitator.

Project facilitators should be equipped with all the skills they need for leading the team to success.

4 Team Leader

Successful project management requires selecting the right *team leader*, generally a Maverick who would spend three months working 50 percent of his or her time on the project redesign. This person consistently shows natural leadership and good project management skills.

The selection of the right team leader can make or break a team.

The selection of the team leader is critical because it can make or break a team. If the team leader is not up to the challenge, problems will arise. Some warning signals include projects falling behind schedule and members missing meetings.

Projects that succeed despite having a weak team leader do so because the facilitator often steps into the void, or because the team or corporate steering committee realizes a mistake has been made and changes the leader.

The Redesign Team 5

The *redesign team* consists of Mavericks. This is because you must have your best people in the redesign of the process. **The caliber of the people will dictate the caliber of the result.** Mavericks are the people who every day get the job done and overcome the obstacles. They really know how a process works and what it takes to produce the result. Although it is hard to pull out your Mavericks from the daily business to work on process redesign, it must be viewed as a short-term loss for a long-term gain.

Finally another word of caution: A popular practice adopted by many organizations is to financially reward redesign teams by enticing them with a percentage of the savings. This dangerous practice should be avoided. The team often calculates the expected bonus and is then hugely disappointed when the financial department calculates a different number. This leads to disappointment rather than motivation. In addition, successful implementation of the changed process is the job of everyone it touches, not just the redesign team—yet what incentive or reward do the rest of the employees receive?

Avoid financially rewarding redesign teams with a percentage of the expected savings.

A team member in a certain company led a project for six months on top of her normal duties. At the end of the successful redesign project, she received $200 as a small token of the organization's appreciation. But instead of valuing the reward, she was shocked. She turned to her colleague on the team and asked sarcastically, "Is that how much the company values our efforts?"

Instead of recognizing her efforts and rewarding them effectively, the organization had inadvertently insulted her with that sum.

A more thoughtful reward, a token in kind such as a DVD player or a weekend away, would have been more effective. Both items cost about the same as the cash reward and would focus on recognizing the team leader's efforts in a way she would appreciate more than cash. Money can be used to reward good performance but small amounts simply disappear into a wallet or purse without really being noticed and may be seen as offensive. Ironically, however, a carefully selected gift of only minimum value can create the desired motivational effect.

 BEST PRACTICE #7
Provide the support infrastructure for the redesign team.

Summary

This chapter has focused on the importance of congruence between what you *say* you are going to do and what you actually *do*. Process alignment is about focusing on the way you work and looking for improvements. To make improvements, don't struggle to reinvent the wheel. Instead, adopt the best practices available in the marketplace (unless your strategy is to be a world-class process leader—in which case you must innovate rather than copy) and learn from other organizations' successes and failures.

Obsolete yourself or the competition will.
Lew Platt, ex-CEO, Hewlett Packard

Have you ever noticed that solutions to problems are always the things you try last?
Anonymous

In the final analysis, you can't continue to reduce costs and grow.
Paul Cook, Founder, Raychem

No business can cut its way to success.
Bill Dahlberg, Chairman, The Southern Company

One doesn't discover new lands without consenting to lose sight of the shore for a very long time.
Andre Gide (1869-1951)

When you have eliminated the impossible that which remains, however improbable, must be the truth.
Arthur Conan Doyle, Creator of Sherlock Holmes

Reducing the cost of quality is in fact an opportunity to increase profits without raising sales, buying new equipment, or hiring new people.
Philip Crosby, Author and Quality Guru

- Implementing strategy means reviewing the current processes and aligning them toward the new desired results.

- Don't reinvent the wheel when you can learn and adopt best practices from others who have gone before you.

- Not every process must or should be operating at Six Sigma.

- Process redesign is about changing the way we work. To change a process, you must change what the people do.

- The larger the scope of the redesign, the more time the redesign team must dedicate to preparing for the implementation.

- Every process must have the customer at its center and every step must directly or indirectly add value to the customer.

- It's critical to identify customer feedback proactively and not simply rely on customer comments.

- The project champion is responsible for overseeing not only the redesign of the process but also its implementation.

- Don't assume you know what customers want, rather than gather empirical evidence and also use your intuition.

- Project facilitators should be trained with all the skills they need for leading the team to success.

- A key reason why organizations fail to implement strategy successfully is because they don't change their basic ways of operating.

- Poor processes in an organization negatively affect customers in the long run.

- When creating measures for your implementation, carefully consider whether percentages will produce the true picture.

- Organizations can fail to provide people with the training and tools to assist them when changing processes—and then experience disastrous results.

- By not preparing for the soft side of implementation, you set yourself up for failure—and the team's future too.

- Many organizations do not solicit customer feedback or track customer satisfaction!

- When you start internalizing the voice of the customer, there may be over-enthusiasm in different departments to approach the same customer. As a result, the customer is inundated with requests for the same information.

- The selection of the right team leader can make or break a team.

- Avoid financially rewarding redesign teams with a percentage of the expected savings.

chapter 11

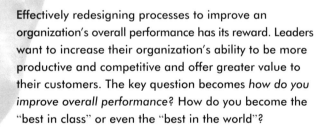

Process
We are Number One

The race is on to finish building the bridge and put processes in place that will boost your organization to the top. But how do you lead it to become number one in your industry?

Effectively redesigning processes to improve an organization's overall performance has its reward. Leaders want to increase their organization's ability to be more productive and competitive and offer greater value to their customers. The key question becomes *how do you improve overall performance*? How do you become the "best in class" or even the "best in the world"?

Organizations perform at different levels and in this chapter, we will examine the different levels—standard, best in class, best in the world and out of this world—and discuss what it takes to improve.

Levels Of Performance

Standard

When you join an organization, you're sometimes given its Standard Operating Procedure (SOP) manual. It may have a different name—such as orientation manual or departmental guidelines. Whatever it's called, the manual indicates how things are done in the organization and what standards you're expected to maintain. It may state, for example, that employees answer the phone within three rings, they must greet customers by name whenever possible, they must respond to voicemail within one working day and so on. These are the standard levels of performance in the organization.

Best in Class

Some organizations, however, are not content being the same as others; they want to achieve a higher level of performance. These organizations operate at the next level, called "best in class". "Best in class" organizations offer a level of performance higher than their competitors. They stand alone among them as doing things better, faster and more efficiently.

Best in The World

A smaller number of organizations are not content even with being "best in class." These organizations strive to become *best in the world*. They offer not just a higher level of performance compared to their competition but also a higher level of performance compared to organizations in other industries anywhere in the world.

Best in the world organizations set a level of performance that sometimes redefines their industry. Their people are frequently the innovators of tomorrow. They are the organizations people admire, talk about and want to work for. Some of these organizations include Singapore Airlines, Sony and Microsoft.

Out of this World

Then there are the rare times an organization performs to a standard that's simply *out of this world!*

This level is rarely reached and hard to maintain, because today's excellence becomes tomorrow's standard. These organizations set standards that will be the envy of not just their competitors but of other organizations. They completely reshape their industries. For example, consider this—yesterday's standard for traveling between Hong Kong and London was 13 weeks by boat. For its time, this was a "best in the world" standard. Today, we fly between Hong Kong and London in 13 hours. In the future, we'll travel between Hong Kong and London in less than an hour! How? On a space ship. We'll go up into orbit in Hong Kong and come back down in London, all within an hour! Feasible? Certainly, that's no more extreme than telling people 100 years ago that the standard traveling time will shrink from 100 days to 13 hours by moving at 800 kilometers an hour in the air!

Today's excellence becomes tomorrow's standard.

Remember, standards are not static; they are like moving escalators. After all, the speed limit in New York City was only eight miles an hour in 1895! Some would even argue that the driving speed has not changed!

One More Level...

What do we call the level of performance that's below standard? You may be thinking "substandard"—but that does not do justice to the description.

When an organization promises to deliver a certain standard and drops below it, then it's "criminal"—it's criminal to make a promise or put in place a service level agreement and then not deliver to that standard.

OUT OF THIS WORLD
BEST IN THE WORLD
BEST IN CLASS
STANDARD
CRIMINAL!

Take a moment to determine at which level you would rate your organization.

It's criminal to make a promise and then not deliver to that standard.

Moving on Up

More often than not, when an organization starts to implement strategy, it wants to move itself up the performance escalator. How does an organization move from standard to "best in class" or even "best in the world"? Let's take a closer look at the challenge of moving on up the performance escalator.

Standards are always rising. An organization must keep improving to keep pace or move ahead.

From Standard to Best in Class

Benchmarking

OUT OF THIS WORLD
BEST IN THE WORLD
BEST IN CLASS
STANDARD
CRIMINAL!

Catch-up Strategy

To move from standard to best in class, you can learn from others by benchmarking. Benchmarking is fast becoming a common practice among organizations because it's a cost-effective, highly impactful and relatively fast way to improve performance. It is, however, often applied only to businesses in the same industry.

Benchmarking your competition will not make you number one in your industry.

This is a mistake if you want your organization to be number one in your industry, as the following example explains.

Company A is a fast food restaurant currently operating at the level shown in the diagram for kitchen hygiene. It wants to improve its performance, but what organization can it benchmark against?

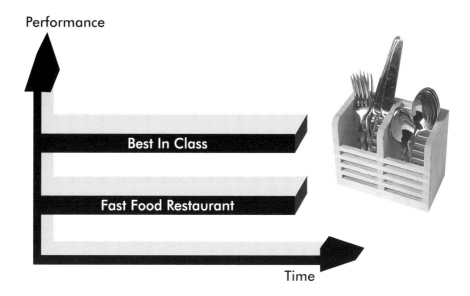

It selects McDonald's, a leader in the fast food industry.
If Company A benchmarks against McDonald's level of hygiene, will it:

1. **Overtake McDonald's level?**
2. **Be at the same level?**
3. **Be at a lower level?**

After benchmarking, it will still have a lower level of hygiene performance because McDonald's does not rest at its current level of performance; it's always improving. Therefore, by the time Company A reaches McDonald's performance level, McDonald's has already moved on to a higher level.

The goal of benchmarking is typically to improve performance so your organization performs better than its competitors. But under this strategy, it can never become "best in class" because it always lags behind. The organization is always playing catch up to your competition. In reality, the organization is adopting a **catch–up strategy** as it constantly tries to meet the standard set by the competition. (See following diagram.)

Kitchen Hygiene

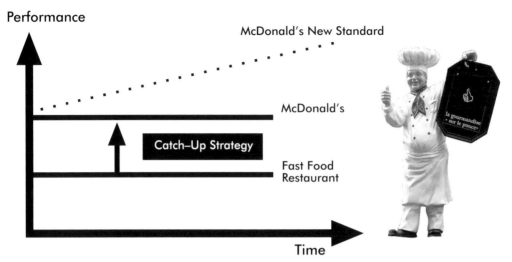

Performance

McDonald's New Standard

McDonald's

Catch–Up Strategy

Fast Food
Restaurant

Time

A catch-up strategy refers to the situation in which companies constantly lag behind the competition, trying to close the gap but never quite succeeding.

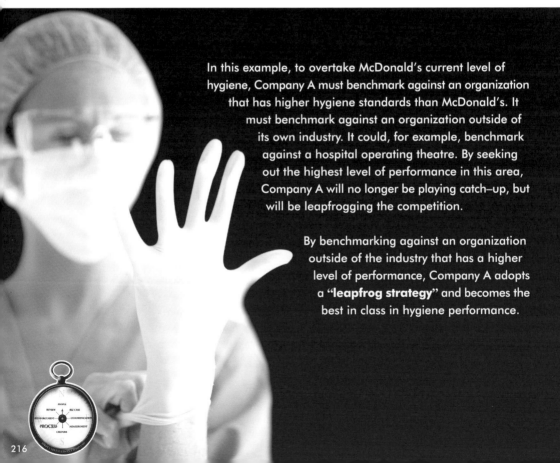

In this example, to overtake McDonald's current level of hygiene, Company A must benchmark against an organization that has higher hygiene standards than McDonald's. It must benchmark against an organization outside of its own industry. It could, for example, benchmark against a hospital operating theatre. By seeking out the highest level of performance in this area, Company A will no longer be playing catch–up, but will be leapfrogging the competition.

By benchmarking against an organization outside of the industry that has a higher level of performance, Company A adopts a **"leapfrog strategy"** and becomes the best in class in hygiene performance.

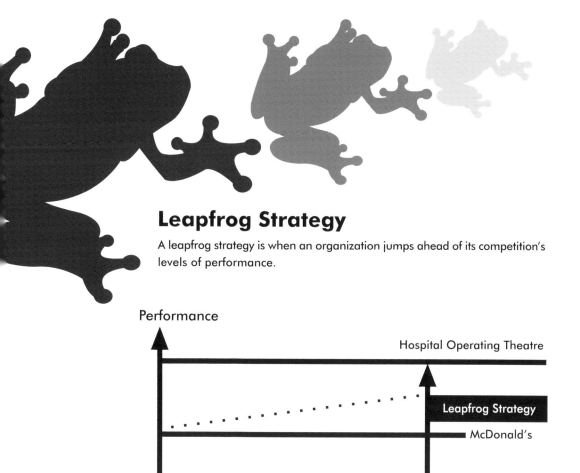

Leapfrog Strategy

A leapfrog strategy is when an organization jumps ahead of its competition's levels of performance.

Performance

Hospital Operating Theatre

Leapfrog Strategy

McDonald's

Fast Food Restaurant

Time

When Singapore obtained its independence, the then Prime Minister Lee Kuan Yew had a tough challenge to generate work and build the country's infrastructure. To create jobs, the fledging nation tried manufacturing many different products including toothbrushes, toothpaste and mosquito coils. Addressing senior executives of French communications giant Publicis at its regional conference in June 2003, Mr. Lee told the audience that, in the first few years, it settled for two strategies. The first was to leapfrog the region by attracting multi-national companies into Singapore and the second was to make Singapore a first-world oasis in what was then a third-world region. Mr. Lee went on to say, "The key to success long before I learned about differentiating products was to make Singapore different. I knew if we were the same as the rest, we had no chance. This did not depend just on infrastructure, but also changing people to live and behave like first-world citizens."

Organizations playing catch-up can be found in some of airports in Asia Pacific where a fiercely competitive battle is on to become Asia's premier hub.

A few years ago, Hong Kong moved its airport to Lantau Island, a 45-minute drive from downtown Hong Kong. To make it easy for passengers to access the airport or travel downtown, authorities built an express train that takes 23 minutes to go between the airport and downtown Hong Kong. The train is very clean and easy to use. It runs every 15 minutes.

Shortly after Hong Kong introduced its express train, Singapore extended its mass railway transit system to offer train services from the airport to downtown Singapore in 30 minutes. The trains run about every 10 minutes.

Shortly after Singapore and Hong Kong introduced their new train services, Malaysia did the same thing at its international airport outside Kuala Lumpur. In just 28 minutes, you can take an express train from the airport to Kuala Lumpur. It runs about every 15 minutes.

Shortly after Hong Kong, Singapore and Malaysia implemented their train services, Shanghai introduced its magnetic levitation train, which runs at speeds of 430 kilometers an hour and takes people from the airport to downtown Shanghai in only eight minutes. It is the first of its kind in commercial operation in the world.

In each case, the other airports have been using a catch-up strategy with Hong Kong—but you could say that Shanghai has made a play at becoming "best in the world" by leapfrogging over the competition.

Another example of a leapfrog strategy in action comes from Southwest Airlines. Southwest Airlines is an organization many people consider to be "best in the world" at what it does, but it began with just a "standard" level of performance.

Southwest Airlines identified that a critical performance area for the organization was the time it took one of its planes to turn around once it arrived at the airport gate. "Turnaround" of an aircraft includes unloading the passengers and luggage, refueling and cleaning the plane, completing the pre-flight checks with the pilot and then loading the new luggage and finally the passengers.

Southwest wanted to shorten this turnaround time as much as possible. To do so, it could have benchmarked against Northwest or United Airlines—but then it would have been playing catch-up.

So what did Southwest Airlines choose to benchmark against?

An Indy 500 motor racing pit stop team.

Why?

Southwest Airlines wanted to leapfrog the competition. Today, Southwest Airlines has the fastest turnaround of aircraft in the industry—15 minutes. That's how much time it normally takes most airlines to unload the flight, never mind have the new passengers board the plane and take off again.

When they benchmark, organizations should isolate the process they want to benchmark and then identify the best organization at that process, no matter which industry it comes from.

12 Steps to Benchmarking

To benchmark a process, an organization can follow these steps:

ONE

Identify and select benchmarking organization

First, identify the specific process that needs to be improved, then identify the organization to benchmark against. For example, Xerox (the organization that created benchmarking) wanted to improve its billing to customers, so it began benchmarking its process against American Express. (Have you ever noticed that your credit card bill always arrives on time?) Remember, when selecting the organization to benchmark against, look outside of your own industry for the organization that excels in the specific area you want to improve. The organization you select may not excel overall, but must excel in your specified area.

TWO

Identify the data to be collected and the format required

In preparing to meet the external organization, be clear on the data to be collected and its format for comparison. What do you need to know? Do you want to examine, for example, cycle time or innovation or R&D? Do you want to see a process map or spread sheets?

THREE

Identify a steering committee and key players

To implement the benchmarking process, ensure you have the support of the steering committee. The steering committee's role is not to approve or disapprove the team's work but to guide it and clear any roadblocks.

FOUR

Gather internal baseline data and external organization data

Gather the internal baseline data and then gather the data from the external organization. It's critical to have the internal baseline data so you can:
- measure where you are today.
- set realistic future performance levels.
- measure the level of improvement.

FIVE

Analyze gaps

Compare the current performance levels with the benchmarked process to identify how the process can be improved. Many teams at this stage recommend adding more people to the process or buying better technology but these solutions aren't necessarily the best if you're striving for a strong ROI.

SIX

Predict future performance levels

Based on the research gathered to date, the team is now in a position to predict future performance levels. The acceptable levels are unique to each organization, depending on the organization's current strategy and how aggressive its leaders want to be.

SEVEN

Generate potential solutions

Once you know what you need to achieve, how will you do it? Team members work together to identify several potential solutions. The purpose of generating more than one solution is to identify the best solution, not just the first one that comes to mind.

EIGHT
Select the best solution

With inputs from the project champion and the team's collective knowledge, you can now decide on the best approach for successful implementation of the new way of working.

NINE
Present solution to steering committee (for support not permission)

The main purpose of presenting the solution is to gain the support and guidance of the steering committee while ensuring your solution aligns with organization direction and strategy. Again, the steering committee's role is to advise and support the team, not give permission. It has already empowered the team to conduct the benchmarking.

TEN
Confirm the action plan

At this stage it's beneficial to revisit the action plan and confirm duties for implementation. Team members are each responsible for different action items.

ELEVEN
Implement action plans

This is the toughest step because it:
- involves changing the way the business operates.
- involves the most people.
- takes the greatest amount of time.

To ensure that the implementation stays on track, the team conducts monthly audits.

TWELVE
Evaluate results

Once the process is complete, results will be reviewed, teams rewarded and successes celebrated.

From "Best In Class" to "Best In The World"

As organizations move up the levels of performance, some set their sights on becoming best in the world. This is not an easy step and (as we have discussed) benchmarking won't get you there: it will only make you as good as the organizations with which you have compared yourself.

So to move from "best in class" to "best in the world,"
the organization must...innovate.

Innovate

OUT OF THIS WORLD
BEST IN THE WORLD
BEST IN CLASS
STANDARD
CRIMINAL!

Innovation, in a nutshell, is breaking the traditional pattern of working by doing things differently. Innovation has propelled many organizations from oblivion to center stage, simultaneously changing the rules for the whole industry and making the organization the best around.

Here are a few examples of organizations (and an individual) who have rewritten the rules in their industry and successfully come out on top.

To be best in the world...Innovate.

Shouldice Hospital

Have you ever heard of the Shouldice Hospital just outside Toronto in Canada? The Shouldice Hospital exemplifies how to be innovative and become the "best in the world." It has segmented its customer market and developed a strategy that's a model of excellence.

Shouldice Hospital doctors perform more operations than in other hospitals (more than 600 a year), but are paid less than other doctors. The doctors are rarely on call and therefore, are available to see their children grow up. The hospital spends less money on equipment than the average hospital. The patients recover in a shorter period (instead of five to eight days, they are released in three to five days) and the nurses handle more patients than most hospitals.

Shouldice Hospital doesn't even look like a hospital because it's located on a country club estate that's conducive to outdoor exercise. Indeed, it doesn't even smell like a hospital (it uses disinfectants that are odorless) or feel like a hospital (its floors are carpeted).

Hospital leaders manage it by being innovative in the way they segment its business and customers. Specifically, it only conducts one kind of operation: hernias (and only one kind of hernia: inguinal). You read that right—it only conducts one kind of operation! This policy allows their doctors and nurses to become highly specialized.

When patients arrive, the check-in time is minimized and the surgeon who will operate the next day examines them. Patients then carry their own bags to a shared room. Patients even have to shave themselves in preparation for the operation. Other patients counsel incoming patients, sometimes within hours of their own operation and all patients are held responsible for their own recovery.

The doctors and nurses believe that the fastest way to recover from a hernia operation is to walk around. Therefore before their operations, patients must walk themselves down to the operating theater. There are no orderlies and no wheelchairs.

Surgeons at Shouldice have invented a special technique for hernia operations. In fact, they've become so specialized, they can perform it without using a general anesthetic. Instead, they use a local anesthetic, which means that the doctors operate while patients are awake. During an operation, it's likely that nurses will chat with their patients about their family and children.

When an operation is complete, patients walk back to their rooms themselves.

Over the next few days, the hospital encourages them to walk around and speed up their recovery time. If they want to watch TV, patients have to walk to the communal TV room. They can't order room service for their meals; they have to walk with their drips to the communal dining room.

Statistics show that patients at Shouldice recover in half the time taken by patients undergoing the same operation at other hospitals. The hospital has also gained an excellent reputation for the care the doctors and nurses give their patients. The patients are so pleased with the hospital's service that, a few years ago, they hosted a reunion of "alumni." Amazingly, 1,500 people showed up at the reunion. You can just imagine the dinner conversation: "I bet my scar is smaller than yours!"

Shouldice Hospital has become the "best hospital in the world" for hernia operations by applying innovation to what it does.

FedEx

Another organization that became the "best in the world" through innovation is FedEx.

When Fred Smith began the organization, no one had heard of this new start-up called Federal Express, named after their first client, the Fed. He had a vision of an organization that could deliver parcels overnight instead of taking three to four days. While he was studying at Yale University in the 1970s, he even wrote a paper about his vision. His professor gave the paper a "C" with the comment that Fred's idea was good in principle but wouldn't work in the real world.

Today, FedEx is built around its credo: absolutely overnight delivery guaranteed. It enjoys a reputation worldwide for delivering as promised—something many organizations do not.

It took a while, however, for FedEx to soar. After Smith returned from the Vietnam War in 1971, he was running a small aviation organization. He discovered that spare parts ordered for his aircraft took a long time to be delivered, sometimes as long as four days. This was frustrating to Smith and other organization owners. From this, he recognized the opportunity to put his college thesis into practice and started a small package delivery service. In the early days, he struggled to make an impression competing against more than 250 other parcel delivery companies in the United States. The first day in operation, for example, FedEx delivered six parcels, one of which Smith sent himself!

His idea, however, of delivering parcels overnight by flying them all into a central hub, sorting them by their destinations, then flying them out just a few hours later started to catch on. FedEx became the "best in the world" through its innovative way of delivering parcels.

Dell

Michael Dell rewrote the way PCs were distributed to customers. Starting in his dorm room at college, he began eliminating the middleman and sold computers directly to end-users.

Dell identified that customers wanted reliable, low-cost computers. He determined that the purchase process was a secondary concern; people would be content to receive their computer through the mail. With this single realization, he built an organization with a market value of around two billion dollars and won market share from the "big boys" in the industry as a start-up organization. Dell delivered quality and reliability at affordable prices. On top of that, he further enhanced brand image by offering a customer service hotline that quickly and efficiently dealt with 90 percent of all calls. Dell has become "best in the world" in the assembly and delivery of computers. Today, the organization sells its expertise to organizations in non-competing industries.

Starbucks

What Michael Dell did for computers, Howard Schultz did for coffee. Around the time Dell was pondering a better way to assemble and deliver computers, Schultz was in Italy buying coffee for a small organization called Starbucks Coffee Co. While walking through the streets of Italy, Schultz noticed that people would start their day by stopping off at a coffee shop on the way to work. The coffee shops were clean and gave off a pleasant aroma that would whet the appetite of passing coffee drinkers. Schultz decided to import not only the coffee but also the coffee shop concept to America.

He quit his job because his bosses wouldn't support this idea. After pounding the pavement to raise enough capital, he opened his first café in Seattle in 1986 and started serving Starbucks coffee.

Coffee drinkers who had been thirsty for variety in their choice of coffee swarmed to the new innovative concept of gourmet coffee and cafés. The price difference between the coffees purchased from the vending machine in a polystyrene cup and the cost of a real latté from freshly ground beans became negligible as coffee drinkers appreciated the taste and the atmosphere.

Starbucks now has over 6,000 stores in more than 30 countries, with three new stores opening every day. It has even recently made the Fortune 500 list.

Dick Fosbury (bet that name got you!)

At the 1968 Olympics in Mexico City, a young American athlete Dick Fosbury—the first high jumper to approach and clear the bar backwards—won gold and set a new Olympic record. Many of those watching shook their heads in disbelief at his technique, the Fosbury Flop. Yet, within a few years, all high jump competitors had switched to this new technique because anyone who decided to stick with the conventional "straddle" style could no longer keep up with the world's best.

To reach new heights of performance as Dick Fosbury did, leaders need new, unconventional ideas—they need innovation—and this applies to both sports and business.

Other Innovators

Other organizations that have captured market share and become recognized as best in the world include Nordstrom's (customer service), the Home Depot (product range), Toys R Us (product range), Microsoft (product innovation) and Singapore Airlines (service and the Singapore Girl).

Characteristics of a best in the world Organization

The best in the world organization is not necessarily the best in every category of its value chain. For example, FedEx is excellent at delivering packages overnight but isn't considered best in the world for customer service. Seven characteristics of a best in the world organization are:

1. **Global Recognition**
2. **Excellence in One Key Area Only**
3. **Full Systems and Structure Support**
4. **High Value Creation**
5. **High Ethics**
6. **Strong People and High Morals**
7. **Social Responsibility**

1. Global Recognition

Others recognize your organization as the leader or benchmark. The "best in the world" organizations don't give themselves this title; it comes from customers or other organizations.

2. Excellence in One Key Area Only

Typically, organizations excel in only one key area, such as Singapore Airlines excelling in customer service. Though competent in the other areas of the business, it's considered "best in the world" in only one. Paradoxically, once the branding of "best in the world" is applied to this one area, it tends to spill over into the whole organization.

3. Full Systems and Structure Support

When one part of a business excels, it doesn't do so at a cost to another part of the business. The organization ensures that the other parts of the business still perform at a high standard and doesn't suffer because of the focus on the area in which it excels.

4. High Value Creation

"Best-in-the-world" organizations create long-term value for their shareholders and show strong leading and lagging indicators of performance over the long run.

5. High Ethics

The way the organization conducts itself is of the highest standards. The organization takes full accountability for its actions and is transparent in its dealings.

6. Strong People and High Morals

The people hired to work for "best in the world" organizations are mostly top performers with high values or morals. Top performers are attracted to the organization because of its excellence and vice versa.

7. Social Responsibility

These organizations are conscious not only of what they do internally but also externally.

For example, McDonald's is very supportive of the communities in which it has a presence. It's an organization that's conscious of looking after the impact it has on the environment its people work in.

To innovate is not to reform.
Edmund Burke

To stay ahead you must have your next idea waiting in the wings.
Rosabeth Moss Kanter

Incrementalism is innovation's worst enemy.
Nicholas Negroponte

Imagination is intelligence having fun.
Anonymous

What is now proved was once only imagined.
William Blake

If there is no struggle there is no progress.
Frederick Douglas

- Standards are always rising. An organization must keep improving to keep pace or move ahead.

- When they benchmark, organizations should isolate the process they want to benchmark and then identify the best organization at that process, no matter which industry it comes from.

- To be best in the world...Innovate.

- Today's excellence becomes tomorrow's standard.

- It's criminal to make a promise and then not deliver to that standard.

- Benchmarking your competition will not make you number one in your industry.

- A catch-up strategy refers to the situation in which companies constantly lag behind the competition, trying to close the gap but never quite succeeding.

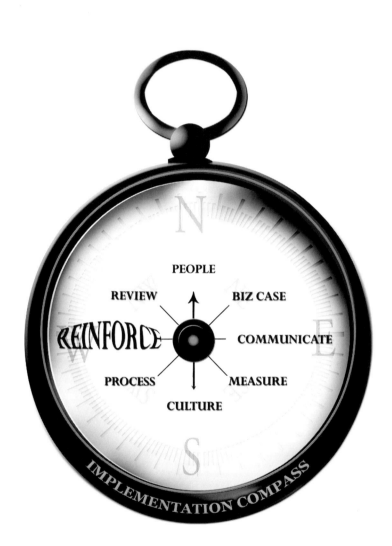

chapter 12

Reinforce
Always Reinforce what you Want

You can reinforce behavior with a teddy bear or simply a pat on the back. But always reinforce the actions you want as a way to encourage people to keep building the bridge.

It's not the organization that crosses the bridge, it is the people. To reinforce their efforts; be sure to recognize and reward them.

At the end of the day, it is the people who have taken the action to implement the strategy. It is the people who make the difference. You can build a better mousetrap or copy a delivery system. But the people in the organization can't be reverse-engineered or simply copied (at least as long as cloning people is illegal!).

Double your investment in your people; the rewards will exceed that investment.

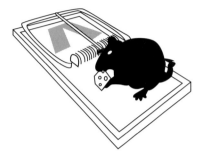

Chapter 4 introduced the four characteristics of the way people respond to change. Here's how they behave:

Mavericks
Positive thinkers, action oriented and committed to the change

Groupies
Followers who avoid the spotlight and are generally content in their jobs

Saboteurs
Negative, destructive and complain about anything and everything

Double Agents
Cautious, skeptical observers who could give or withdraw their support

In an ideal world, all staff members would be Mavericks. Unfortunately, reality is very different.

Let's take a closer look at Mavericks and examine one of their characteristics in more detail—their commitment to change. This will allow you to understand how you can create more Mavericks in your organization.

It is often said that the soft stuff is the hard stuff. Implementing strategy requires one-third logic and two-thirds emotion.

Gaining Commitment

A distinguishing characteristic of Mavericks is their high level of commitment to change compared with the other three categories. (It's worth noting that Saboteurs can also have high levels of commitment, but for the wrong reasons—they are highly committed to seeing implementation fail!).

An examination of the rationale for Mavericks' high commitment to change also helps us explain:

Why some people go on a diet and successfully lose weight while others diet but can't keep the weight off.

Why some people are able to give up smoking while others cannot.

Why some people live healthily and others cannot.

Why some people can go home at a reasonable time from the office and have dinner with their families, while others cannot.

To understand what makes the difference, let's examine what lies beneath this commitment and look at the different levels.

Levels of Commitment

People bring different levels of

commitment to a project when

adopting a change and these levels

can vary, depending on the situation.

They are commonly reflected in the

terms; Wishers, Hopers, Likers, Tryers

and Wanters. How do these behavior

groups differ from each other?

⚔ **Wishers** ⚔

The lowest level of commitment to a change is communicated through those who say "I wish." On New Year's Eve at five minutes to midnight, wishers would say, "My New Year's resolution is to stop smoking" and two hours later, they're enjoying a cigarette. They've totally forgotten about their resolution and they almost always fail to see their changes materialize. They do little more than utter those two words and take no action to change anything.

⚔ **Hopers** ⚔

At the next level of commitment (one up above Wishers) are people who say, "I hope." Hopers recognize that they need to take action, but just the thought of having to do that is enough to discourage them from taking it.

Hopers would say, "I hope to give up smoking but I really enjoy a cigarette when I'm having a drink with friends (or when I feel stressed)." Most Hopers fail to make the change they say they want because they associate too much pain with taking action.

⚔ **Likers** ⚔

Moving up the ladder of commitment are those who say, "I would like to..." These people would sincerely like to make a change "because …" and they state a good reason. For example, they would say, "I would like to lose weight because I will feel better about myself."

All but a handful, however, of Likers will fail because the benefits of changing aren't strong enough for them to alter their patterns of behavior.

⚔ **Tryers** ⚔

Then, there are those who say, "I will try." Sound familiar? Tryers identify the action they need to take and go as far as setting a date to take the action. Yet, most Tryers fail because, even though they set the date, they still don't take the action. They say, "I am going to try and lose weight and I will start on Monday."

Tryers fail because they never actually take action. They come close; they at least set a date to start. But most never get to the starting line.

⚔ **Wanters** ⚔

The penultimate group, the Wanters, say, "I want to give up smoking." This group comes close to success. Some may even succeed in making their changes happen, but even here, most will fail because of one little word that comes after "I want." That word is but.

They say, "I want to give up smoking but I am up for promotion and I am under so much pressure." Or "I want to lose weight but I am attending a conference and there's so much food available at breaks and lunches." Wanters come up with every excuse known about why they cannot do something.

Why do Wishers, Hopers, Likers, Tryers and Wanters fail while people such as Mavericks are able to make the right levels of commitment? People who are commited...

Think Pleasure!

Mavericks, for example, associate more pleasure with the result of making the change rather than the pain of taking the action. To continue the smoking example, people who succeed at stopping to smoke do so because they associate more pleasure with being healthy, living a longer life and seeing their grandchildren than with the pain of withdrawal they will experience when they stop smoking.

People who are successful in making changes are fully committed to the change because they associate more benefits with the change than with staying as they are.

Here are more examples:

Clean-Shaven Men

How many guys enjoy shaving? Not many; in fact, some grow beards to avoid the pain of shaving and others would happily go around with a five o'clock shadow. Many men shave because they gain more pleasure from looking presentable and conforming to society's preference for a clean-shaven look than they do the pain of shaving. Research reported in local Singapore papers even stated that clean-shaven men have sex more often than unshaven men. Now, that's evidence of more pleasure.

When the pleasure outweighs the pain, people take action. They become committed.

Women and High Heels

Why do women wear high-heeled shoes? If you ask them if these shoes are the most comfortable pair in their wardrobe, most will say no. Why, then, do they select a pair of uncomfortable shoes over a more comfortable pair?

They choose high-heeled shoes because they get more pleasure from looking and feeling good, compared with the discomfort and pain from wearing the shoes. They tell themselves, "More gain, less pain!" Some research claims women even feel sexier while wearing high-heeled shoes.

Dieters and Discipline

Some people can go on a diet and lose weight while others can't—an example best illustrated in the story of *The Wedding Portrait*.

The Wedding Portrait

Imagine the situation: the bride-to-be is having afternoon tea with her friends in the local hotel two weeks before her wedding. The waiter wheels the dessert trolley over to the table. He makes a big show of removing the cover to reveal the chocolate cake, the cream éclairs, the double-layered strawberry sponge and asks the bride, "Would madam care for dessert?" Though her head is nodding yes, she manages to say, "No, thank you" to the waiter.

How does she manage to resist the temptation? How at that moment is she able to control her desire?

It is because she is thinking of her wedding portrait.

She is thinking of the moment when her family and friends hear the celebrant pronounce them married.

She is thinking of walking with her husband back up the aisle towards the large mahogany doors and as the doors open, there waiting outside is the photographer—the photographer who will take the wedding portrait that is going to sit on their television set for *the rest of their lives!*

The wedding portrait that their friends will look at. The wedding portrait that the whole family will ask to see.

The wedding portrait that a few years later the children will look at and say, "Mummy, you were so beautiful on your wedding day!"

The wedding portrait that the grandchildren will see and say, "Grandma, were you really that thin once?"

It is these thoughts that allow the bride to say no to the waiter. The bride associates more pleasure with looking good in the wedding portrait than she associates with the pain of missing out on a delicious but fattening dessert.

Some people manage to **exercise six days a week** while others feel lucky to manage six days a year, in spite of their stated desire to do so. Those who exercise frequently obtain more pleasure from being fit than pain from doing the exercises. For many, however, the short-term pleasure of skipping exercise to lie longer in bed or to eat junk food outweighs the long-term pain of feeling tired or not eating the right food. (A classic fast food meal is saturated with trans fat, which contribute to numerous diseases, including cancer. It is high in calories, low on vitamins and minerals, a poor source of protein and high in processed carbs, which may lead to type-2 diabetes.)

What about those who stay at work late instead of going home? Just remember when you spend your evenings working rather than being with your family, you're communicating that the pleasure of being in the office is greater than the pain of missing your family. Many people struggle with the balance between work and leisure.

You can stop that struggle by being clear about what you're committed to.

Think Pleasure
at Work

How does *think pleasure* apply to implementing a process?

For staff members to commit to a change, they must see more pleasure than pain in that change. Your communication strategy must embrace that challenge.

First, it is critical that staff members understand the reason for change (the biz case) and can visualize an outcome that is better than the "no-change" option.

They must also understand how they will benefit (the WII-FM—What's In It For Me.) When people associate pleasure with the change, they will start to commit to it. Different staff members will commit at different times, just as when they are finding their way through the maze, some will give up while others will keep going.

If you want staff members to commit to a change, they must recognize more pleasure than pain in making that change.

Rewards and Recognition

Once people on your staff have given their commitment to implement the strategy and start taking the right action, it is vital they are recognized for their efforts especially when they demonstrate the right behaviors. Some surveys reveal that over 60 percent of U.S. workers say they received no meaningful rewards or recognition for their efforts last year. Over 70 percent of workers consider themselves "disengaged"—clockwatchers who can't wait to go home. To clarify the difference between rewards and recognition, "rewards" are considered financial acknowledgments while "recognition" is considered non-financial. Anything that affects an individual's pay such as an increase in salary is a "reward." Other forms of benefits—from a pat on the back to a new office— can be categorized as "recognition." Because rewards affect people's wages, they must be regarded with sensitivity. So if your organization lacks internal expertise for redesigning reward systems, consider outsourcing that task. The remainder of this chapter deals with recognition, the non-financial factors.

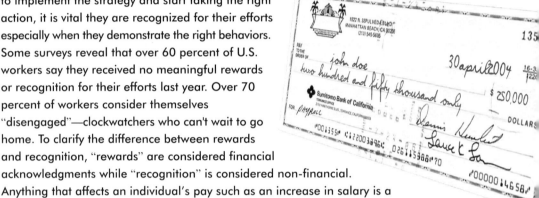

Organizations can't forget to reward and recognize staff over the long journey through the implementation maze.

Cognitive Dissonance

In 1957, Stanford social psychologist Leon Festinger published his theory of cognitive dissonance. Cognitive dissonance is the distressing mental state that arises when people find their beliefs are inconsistent with their actions (for example, an agnostic priest). Through his research, Festinger observed a need to eliminate cognitive dissonance by changing either one's actions or beliefs. For an organization, this finding implies that if people believe in the organization's overall purpose, they'd be happy to change their individual behavior to serve that purpose. Therefore, to feel comfortable with change and to carry it out with enthusiasm, they must understand the role of their actions in the unfolding drama. As noted earlier, anyone leading a strategy implementation must clearly communicate the goals to everyone involved so their contributions make sense to them as individuals.

B.F. Skinner

B.F. Skinner is best known for his experiments with rats during the late 1920s and 1930s. He found that he could motivate a rat to complete the boring task of negotiating a maze in two ways: by providing the right incentives (corn to eat at the end of the maze) and by punishing the rat with electrical shock each time it took a wrong turn. Since Skinner's research, a school of thought has emerged that strongly believes that positive reinforcement encourages a behavior, e.g., food at the end of a maze. Negative reinforcement, e.g. the electrical shock, stops a behavior. Therefore, to implement your strategy, you must create positive reinforcement through staff recognition. We can encourage a person by creating the right environment but ultimately, **we are each responsible for our own cognitions!**

Staff Recognition

As staff members start to demonstrate the right behaviors, recognition will encourage them to repeat these behaviors. Recognition can take many forms: a word of praise and encouragement, a pat on the back, an on-the-spot award, even a lollipop. Your objective is to recognize the right behaviors so they'll be repeated.

Recognizing staff members as they start to demonstrate the desired behaviors is critical for the implementation's success.

Money—motivator or not?

During the implementation leaders see certain people (the Mavericks and some Groupies) demonstrate the desired behaviors and they want to provide them with encouragement and reinforcement.

It's tempting to throw money at them as a means of recognition. Money, however, is not considered a good form of recognition.

"In motivation to work, pay is not a positive but a negative."

Frederick Herzberg

As mentioned in Chapter 11, money can be a demotivator not a motivator. Remember, your objective is to encourage people to adopt new behaviors and actions. Motivation expert Frederick Herzberg wrote, "In motivation to work, pay is not a positive but a negative. Feelings of self-improvement, achievement and the desire for the acceptance of greater responsibility are more unimportant than money for persuading people to increase productivity." All this means is that if you go to work and don't receive sufficient pay, you'll be demotivated. As soon as you receive enough pay for the work, however, money ceases to become that motivator.

Review your current recognition program and ensure it aligns with your strategy implementation and encourages the right actions.

Reflect on this for a Moment

If your boss gives you an additional $1,000 a month, would your work performance improve? The next day after your raise, you may work a little harder (but even then, maybe not). Six months later, it is almost certain you will work at the same pace as you did before receiving the additional $1,000.

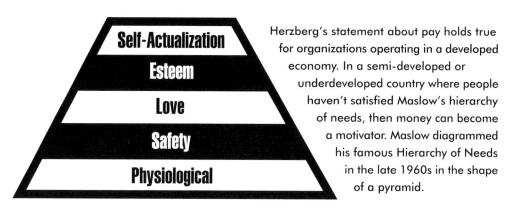

Herzberg's statement about pay holds true for organizations operating in a developed economy. In a semi-developed or underdeveloped country where people haven't satisfied Maslow's hierarchy of needs, then money can become a motivator. Maslow diagrammed his famous Hierarchy of Needs in the late 1960s in the shape of a pyramid.

Maslow Hierarchy of Needs

He believed that as man ascends to higher degrees, his needs change. At the lower level, the needs relate to physiological aspects (e.g., air, water, food, sleep and safety). At the higher levels, mankind's needs change to social interaction and self actualization. According to Maslow, physiological, safety, love and esteem needs must be satisfied before a person can act unselfishly.

In encouraging new behaviors, we have reflected about the importance of recognition and specifically about the benefits of non-financial awards. Many leaders believe money is a good motivator for staff. This, however, is not always the case.

The Benefits of Awards over Cash

When recognizing people, giving them awards has intrinsic and significant benefits over giving them cash because awards can provide an internal feel-good effect that money cannot. A certificate at the end of a course, for example, can represent significant importance to the person who has achieved a new milestone.

Other reasons that awards can be perceived to be better than cash are:

Symbolic awards send a more powerful message and, as such, get discussed among peers.

Awards are immediately associated with the implementation and can help to elevate its importance (whereas cash will disappear through paying bills, taxi fares, etc.).

The value of a non-cash award is increased by what it represents—awards can have a lower financial value than a cash payment, yet provide the same or greater prestige and motivation.

Awards are not interpreted as a taxable benefit whereas money is.

Awards can be personalized to the individual; cash is impersonal.

What motivates people is a sense of purpose.
W. Bennis, Professor and Author

Several research studies have verified that giving an award versus giving cash is advantageous. For example, Walker, Churchill and Ford, 1977, showed that non-monetary incentives act as recognition and that opportunities for professional and personal growth can satisfy many of the manager's psychological needs for gratification. Other research suggests that middle managers use the perceived incentives associated with the strategy implementation as a sign of the importance placed on it by senior management.

Therefore, when implementing your strategy, you need to identify financial and non-financial ways to motivate the staff. In the next section we will examine the relationship between staff members demonstrating the desired behaviors and the consequences *after* they demonstrate the desired behaviors.

Consequences after Taking the Right Action

Recognition provides a positive consequence to staff for adopting the desired new behaviors and taking the right actions. Its consequences can be either:

- **positive or negative**
- **immediate or future**
- **certain or uncertain**

 It's more important for leaders to focus on what they do after staff members demonstrate the behavior (the consequence) than to focus on what happens before.

Let's look at each of these.

Positive or negative

A consequence can be either positive or negative. The person, however, who decides if it's positive or negative is the person receiving the recognition, not the person giving it. Leaders may think they've created the most amazing staff recognition programs, but only its recipients can decide if the program is valued or not. This is because every individual is different; what motivates one person may demotivate another.

  The person who decides if recognition is positive or negative is the person receiving it, not the person giving it.

Consider the popular recognition program of recognizing an employee every month. In many organizations this fails to achieve the desired motivational effect. This is because, typically, the program is the last item on the monthly management meeting agenda. The decision-makers quickly review a handful of names and justifications and then select a winner for that month because they need a name. Then a manager notifies the winner, saying that person will receive a plaque from the CEO at the next town hall meeting in front of the whole organization. In theory, everyone in the organization feels good because management has publicly recognized an individual for outstanding performance.

Some people, however, might feel petrified at the idea of being in the spotlight. As introverts, they desperately want to avoid the public embarrassment of walking across a stage in front of the whole workforce and shaking hands with the CEO. Adding insult to injury, they may not even know why they were nominated. Leaders may be thinking that they are providing a positive consequence for a job well done but they may actually be punishing key members of staff as they do not understand what motivates the individuals. Here is an example: Every year, a bus company recognizes one driver for providing the most outstanding customer service and plasters that person's picture on the outside of a bus. Some drivers might love having their pictures on a side of a bus flashed around the city, but others do not. To find out whether a consequence is positive or negative, ask the employees ahead of time or give them the option to choose their own form of recognition.

To ensure a positive consequence, try this: the next time you have a meeting with your staff, pass out index cards and ask each person to put his or her name on it. Then ask them to list their ten favorite hobbies or pastimes. Collect the cards and continue the meeting without explanation. If anyone asks what the cards are for, just brush the question aside. The next time Sally, one of your team members, demonstrates Maverick qualities and leads the way in implementing the new initiative, look at her index card to see what she would enjoy as a recognition. The next day, present her with, say, the latest and most popular book on photography. The others will be overwhelmed and baffled—how did you know Sally liked photography? They will have forgotten about filling out the index cards. This kind of award gives people like Sally personal, positive recognition—and gives your ratings as leader a boost. It costs very little but its intrinsic value is extremely high.

To find out if a consequence is positive or negative, ask the employees or give them the option to choose their own form of recognition.

Immediate or Future

Receiving recognition can either be immediate or in the future. A good recognition program allows for both.

One of Bridges's clients identified specific behaviors the leaders wanted staff to show as part of a new initiative. Whenever people were seen demonstrating the behavior, they received a small teddy bear to sit on top of their computers. This immediate recognition endorsed the desired behaviors and encouraged them to be repeated. Over the next few months, staff members competed to get the most teddy bears on top of their computers by adopting the new behaviors. Every quarter, management held an additional lucky draw. The number of teddy bears people had earned in the quarter became the equilivant of the number of chances they had in the lucky draw.

Many organizations rely solely on annual appraisals to provide people with their rewards and recognition. The problem with annual appraisals is that they only provide recognition long after the event and are strongly influenced by the *recent-cy* factor.

The recent-cy factor is a pitfall of annual appraisals in which performance over the preceding three months typically has a greater influence than performance over the rest of the year. Therefore, the secret to receiving a good annual appraisal is to focus on the three months before the appraisal and make them the best three months possible!

Annual appraisals don't happen frequently enough to provide good staff feedback.

Certain or Uncertain

A consequence of receiving recognition can be either certain or uncertain. That is, when a new behavior is demonstrated, will people feel certain or uncertain about gaining recognition? As an example, in Singapore, back–seat passengers in cars are required by law to fasten their seatbelts. When the government first introduced the law some years ago, few people wore them, mainly because there was no certainty of punishment. But when police started fining passengers $120 and the driver demerit points, all that changed. Today, everyone wears them because it is more certain they will be caught and fined than before. This gives rise to a question people often ask: "Is it better to provide positive or negative reinforcement?" The answer depends on what you want to achieve. *Positive reinforcement encourages new behaviors; negative reinforcement discourages existing behaviors.*

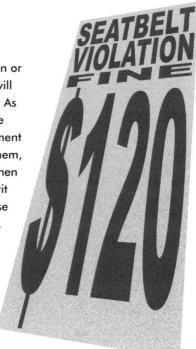

Use positive reinforcement to encourage new behaviors, but use negative reinforcement to discourage existing behaviors.

Negative reinforcement helps people stop "bad" behaviors but it does not encourage them to demonstrate new ones. People use negative reinforcement all the time with children who are told to stop a behavior or avoid an action that will harm them. "Don't touch that; it will burn you!" Positive reinforcement, on the other hand, can encourage a behavior. Taking another example from kids, you might say, "If you are well behaved at the concert, you can have ice cream afterwards."

Aim to strike a balance between certain and uncertain recognition and between positive and negative reinforcement.

Do you remember the Pygmalion effect? According to Greek legend, Pygmalion was a sculptor who fell in love with the statue he had carved of a woman. In answer to his wishes, the statue came to life. For you, the Pygmalion effect is that your staff will deliver what you really believe and expect them to deliver. Bring them to life with your expectation that they will deliver the desired new behaviors!

The Pygmalion effect states that staff members will deliver what you expect them to deliver.

Case Study: Quality Dividends

Citigroup used the concepts discussed in this chapter to develop a quality recognition program across the Asia Pacific operations of its corporate banking group. The program was designed to encourage behaviors that leaders wanted to see in the bank's individuals and teams and to embed them into Citigroup culture. They branded the program Quality Dividends, building on the concept that everyone owns a share of quality. They adopted this theme throughout the recognition program. Quality Dividends aimed to promote behaviors that:

- **go beyond the scope of work expected**
- **satisfy an internal or external customer beyond expectations**
- **motivate, encourage or enhance teamwork**
- **create additional value for Citigroup shareholders**

Citigroup also expected to see outcomes such as financial benefits for the bank. The program was tremendously successful, later being rolled out in the organization across 60 countries and into its private banking operations.

Quality Dividends encourages quality behaviors that ultimately improve customer satisfaction. It built on existing quality initiatives to unite them under a common branding and recognition process. The program had three categories:

1. The Instant Returns Award—singled out actions and behaviors that went beyond the normal scope of work. Given by staff to staff.

2. The Idea Investment Award—encouraged and recognized staff for ideas that demonstrate the potential to lead to business improvements.

3. The Blue Chip Award—recognized the completion of projects that lead to business improvements.

Continuing the dividends theme, Quality Dividends was launched through the Citigroup Quality IPO. Employees received a Quality Dividends Prospectus and an initial number of Quality Shares—the currency of recognition. *Quality Dividends Analysts Reports* were produced throughout the program. To make the recognition program flexible and responsive to individual tastes, participating staff members could choose to redeem their quality shares for awards from four categories:

- **travel**
- **personal/professional**
- **development, entertainment and relaxation**
- **charity donations**

The flexibility to choose your own recognition whenever you wanted to redeem it was a large factor in the program's success. Staff members selected their own form of recognition, which ensured it was seen as positive. They redeemed it whenever they wanted it and they were certain they were going to get it.

Don't aim at success—the more you aim at it and make it a target, the more you are going to miss it. For success, like happiness, cannot be pursued; it must ensue and it only does so as the unintended side effect of one's personal dedication to a cause greater than oneself or as the by-product of one's surrender to a person other than oneself. Happiness must happen and the holds for success: you may have to let it happen by not caring about it.
Victor Frankl, Man's Search for Meaning

To put it another way: it's better to chase your passion than your pension.
Anonymous

Do a job that you love and you will never have to work another day in your life.
Confucius

Work should be more fun than fun!
Anonymous

The want of money is the root of all evil.
Samuel Butler

The quality of life is in the mind, not in the material.
Malcolm Forbes

Unlock your natural drives by doing what you enjoy.
Hans Selye

The key to all motivation is desire and the master key to creating desire is responsiveness to the needs, desires and interests of the people you would lead.
John R. Noe

- Double your investment in your people; the rewards will exceed that investment.

- It is often said that the soft stuff is the hard stuff. Implementing strategy requires one-third logic and two-thirds emotion.

- People who are successful in making changes are fully committed to the change because they associate more benefits with the change than with staying as they are.

- When the pleasure outweighs the pain, people take the action. They become committed.

- If you want staff members to commit to a change, they must recognize more pleasure than pain in making that change.

- Recognizing staff members as they start to demonstrate the desired behaviors is critical for the implementation's success.

- Review your current recognition program and ensure it aligns with your strategy implementation and encouraging the right actions.

- To find out if a consequence is positive or negative, ask the employees or give them the option to choose their own form of recognition.

- Use positive reinforcement to encourage new behaviors but use negative reinforcement to discourage existing behaviors.

- The Pygmalion effect states that staff members will deliver what you expect them to deliver.

- Organizations can't forget to reward and recognize staff over the long journey through the implementation maze

- "In motivation to work, pay is not a positive but a negative."
  Frederick Herzber

- It's more important for leaders to focus on what they do after staff members demonstrate the behavior (the consequence) than to focus on what happens before.

- The person who decides if recognition is positive or negative is the person receiving it, not the person giving it.

- Annual appraisals don't happen frequently enough to provide good staff feedback.

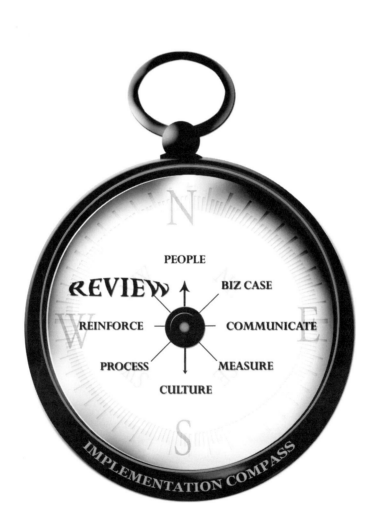

chapter 13

Strategic Implementation Review (SIR)

While traveling across the bridge, keep reviewing your overall implementation.

This vital review ensures you are heading in the right direction, achieving the right results and learning from your mistakes and successes.

Of the eight critical elements on the Implementation Compass, Review is the weakest element as it is the least practiced by leaders. In contrast, when adopted as a business discipline it can mean the difference between success and failure and becomes one of the strongest drivers of the implementation.

The review will make sure that you are doing what you said you were going to do, when you said you were going to do it and that you are creating the right results. In this chapter we discuss the reasons that reviews are so important and the methodology for adopting them.

About Strategic Implementation Reviews
(SIR)

Successful strategy implementation happens when you review the actions being taken periodically and ensure the desired results are being achieved. The process is called Strategic Implementation Review—SIR.

SIR is a two-hour structured meeting conducted regularly by leaders to track their strategy implementation.

By adopting SIR, leaders instill the discipline to ensure that the right actions are being taken and the right results are being achieved. It also provides a platform for reflecting on the overall strategy and making adjustments.

Once you have the fundamentals of your strategy in place, you can start implementing it. Beware that your strategy creation will never be complete for two key reasons: **conditions change and strategies need to be adjusted.**

Conditions Change

It's better to *start* implementing the strategy than wait until you feel you've designed it perfectly. This is because conditions around you will change (such as customer expectations) and the strategy will need to be adjusted accordingly. What was perfect today will not be perfect tomorrow.

A perfect strategy today will not be perfect tomorrow as conditions change.

Strategies Need to be Adjusted

As you start to implement your strategy, you will move from theory to practice, from planning to action and from concept to implementation. As the strategy is rolled out you will realize that what sounded good in theory does not always work in practice and you will need to adjust the strategy accordingly. Adjustment will also need to be made to account for changes in conditions. SIR provides the structure to capture these changes by stepping back every three months and examining your current position relative to your objectives.

Successful strategic implementation results from periodic reviews of actions that ensure that the right results are being achieved.

Follow-through is the DNA of decisive cultures.
Ram Charan, consultant and author

Don't hold meetings longer than two hours; otherwise, they turn into unorganized workshops.

SIR is a very powerful tool that can make the difference between being in the ten percent who succeed or in the 90 percent who fail. The remainder of this chapter will examine:

> 1. **SIR Principles**
> 2. **SIR Objectives**
> 3. **SIR Components**

SIR Principles

The underlying principles of SIR are:
1. Transparency
2. Confidence
3. Responsibility.

1. Transparency

One of the contributing factors to the 1998 Asian financial crisis was the lack of business transparency in many of the countries. People did not know what was happening. This led to a lack of confidence in the currency of some countries.

Similarly, to avoid a lack of confidence in the implementation, leaders must make sure that there is transparency throughout the implementation process. During a period of transition, staff members can become unsure of what to do and may feel nervous about their job security. To ensure transparency, information reported in the reviews must be grounded and have clarity. The content must be accurate, useful and timely. The more open and frank the reviews are, the more efficient and effective they are in accelerating the successful implementation.

Effective leaders follow up with staff members to make sure they did what they said they were going to do.

If the leaders don't have confidence in the numbers reported, they will doubt the implementation and more often than not, they will lose confidence in the whole project.

2. Confidence in the numbers

Reviews are both quantitative and qualitative. It's critical that the numbers reported are accurate. In the reviews, the numbers examined may include increases in revenue, customer satisfaction index, employee satisfaction index and cost reductions. If the leaders don't have confidence in the numbers reported, they will challenge them and start to doubt the implementation. They may also lose confidence in the whole implementation.

One way to increase confidence in the numbers is to use a Management Information System (MIS). This way, the numbers are gathered electronically and the opportunity for human error is reduced. Another best practice is to state all assumptions made before reporting the numbers (e.g., an assumption that the competitions' market share has remained static). Stating assumptions upfront not only helps ensure confidence in the numbers but also reduces debates on how the numbers were calculated, rather than focusing on what they mean to the business.

3. Responsibility for taking the action	A key purpose for SIR is to ensure that those responsible for taking action do so. In fact, it's one of the strongest best practices among effective leaders. An effective leader follows up with staff members to make sure they did what they said they were going to do. SIR starts with a review of actions agreed to be taken from the previous review held.

SIR Objectives

SIR has 10 objectives that aim to:

1 Identify required changes to the implementation and changes in conditions.

2 Ensure effective implementation of actions—SIR tracks actions and more importantly, the results of the actions.

3 Keep the implementation on the senior management's radar screen—there is only so much a leader can focus on. SIR ensures that the strategy implementation remains part of the leadership's long-term focus.

4 Maintain simplicity instead of overcomplicating information. SIR is designed to present relevant information clearly and concisely.

5 Ensure realism in its review and objectives—regular SIRs ensure that leaders constantly check performance against objectives and adjust actions accordingly.

6 Identify additional ideas that emerge as the strategy is implemented.

7 Introduce objectivity into the organizational culture—the discipline of conducting SIR regularly helps ensure that decisions are based on facts and data, as well as intuition.

8 Break down silos—the constant reviewing and sharing of information assists the organization in breaking down silos because leaders and staff improve their understanding of the operating environment, the bigger business picture and the priorities of other departments.

9 Provide constant learning—having a platform for sharing success and learning from mistakes supports the organization's growth.

10 Create long-term organizational success—SIR is instrumental in ensuring that the organization finds its way out of the maze.

SIR Components

The 5 components of SIR are:

1. Review the deliverables.
2. Review the strategic landscape.
3. Assess critical success factors (CSF).
   (This can be achieved by using the "Implementation Cards"–
   see the products at the back of the book.)
4. Document and discuss organizational learning.
5. Plan the next steps.

Let's look at these steps in more detail.

Deliverables

SIR highlights the results of the implementation according to the schedule and the key outcomes of the business. Presenters must clearly explain what's happening (transparency), whether the actions need adjustments and how they will address future challenges. For example, a simple color-coded spreadsheet showing the action items reflects most of this at a glance: Green is on schedule, yellow is an alert to watch carefully and red means trouble.

Strategic Landscape

SIR examines "boardroom trends" that may affect the project. The strategic landscape review looks at stakeholders, organizational changes and environmental analyses. It allows you to keep an eye on the bigger picture and provides the platform for adjustment if the economy or the competition changes.

Critical Success Factors (CSF) Assessment

The CSFs establish the key drivers and challenges that will make or break an implementation, so it is imperative that they are reviewed to acknowledge any impending changes. For example, a common Critical Success Factor in implementation is that leaders maintain focus and lead by example throughout the implementation. The review will check to make sure that they are.

Organizational Learning

In this step, the team documents and discusses key lessons learned during the previous three months of implementation. As the implementation rolls out, different groups will be having different experiences. The review ensures cross-functional group learning so that mistakes are not repeated and best practices are adopted.

Next Step

The review records any changes to the implementation as:

1. Additions—what new action steps need to be taken?

2. Deletions—what should we stop doing?

3. Amendments—what are the changes?

It's just as important to have a "stop" list as a "to do" list.

If required, new owners and deliverable dates are set for each of the changes. After the review, a summary of the outcomes from the SIR should be distributed immediately to keep everyone informed.

> *When you can measure what you are speaking about and express it in numbers, you know something about it; but when you cannot measure it, when you cannot express it in numbers, your knowledge is of a meager and unsatisfactory kind.*
> *Thomas Hurley*

Don't walk out of a meeting without assigning a name to every item that needs follow-up.

Make strategy an everyday act. The creation and re-creation of strategy shouldn't be a process that you undertake only when budgets are due.

- Successful strategic implementation results from periodic reviews of actions that ensure that the right results are being achieved.

- Effective leaders follow up with staff members to make sure they did what they said they were going to do.

- It's just as important to have a "stop" list as a "to do" list.

- Make strategy an everyday act. The creation and re-creation of strategy shouldn't be a process that you undertake only when budgets are due.

- A perfect strategy today will not be perfect tomorrow as conditions change.

- Don't hold meetings longer than two hours; otherwise, they turn into unorganized workshops.

- If the leaders don't have confidence in the numbers reported, they will doubt the implementation and more often than not, they will lose confidence in the whole project.

- Don't walk out of a meeting without assigning a name to every item that needs follow-up.

chapter 14

That's All Folks!

Bricks to Bridges has taken you on a journey through a maze—a metaphor used to describe the challenge of implementing strategy. In doing so, the strategy tells you what you want to achieve and the Implementation Compass makes your strategy come alive.

Implementation involves taking many turns down an indistinct path. It reflects the effort that many people must make, the obstacles they will face and the challenges they need to overcome. It also reflects the excitement that's typical at the start of a new adventure, followed by the dissipation of energy over time.

We first acknowledged that most strategy implementations fail to deliver the desired results—either a new strategy gets introduced or the results' bar is lowered. We rarely, if ever, hear a CEO stand up and declare,

"We just had a strategic failure."

Change the Definition

To assist you through the implementation maze, use the Implementation Compass, a generic tool for guiding you through today's implementation challenges. The compass goes beyond typical implementation to point to what you can do to succeed. It is built on the lessons and experience of previous efforts.

One key component of the Implementation Compass is taking the right action to create the right results. At certain times, however, this is easier said than done—and at other times it is done unintentionally.

On a lighter note, I've compiled a short list of what can happen when organizations have taken the wrong action—called **Business Blunders**.

On a more positive note, what happens when they stumble by accident and achieve the right result—called the **Serendipity Factor**.

BUSINESS
BLUNDERS

one

The Big Mac would never have been part of McDonald's menu if Ray Kroc had gotten his way!

After failures such as the Hulaburger (two slices of cheese and a grilled pineapple ring on a toasted bun—and we're surprised this failed!), Kroc opposed introducing new menu items for a decade.

Money talks, however, and Jim Delligatti, a franchise owner, finally got permission to add the Big Mac to the menu. Within a couple of months of adding the Big Mac, sales jumped 12% and Big Mac got added to the menu at all the McDonald's outlets.

two

In the 1920s, Coca-Cola was invited to buy Pepsi for a modest price. In a very expensive blunder, its leaders rejected the offer.

three

Kleenex tissue was initially sold as a cloth to remove make up; it was never intended as a tissue but it's now sold around the world as one.

four

Levi's® jeans used to have a rivet on the fly until customers wrote in to complain that the rivet was a painfully good conductor of heat when the wearer crouched in front of a campfire.

five

Adidas was approached by an up-and-coming basketball player who loved the company's products and wanted to endorse them.

Nike, a company new on the scene and hungry to hire a promising rookie, offered Michael Jordan $2.5 million for a five-year contract plus royalties on every Air Jordan sold. Adidas offered him $100,000 a year and no royalties. The rest is history.

six

When Alexander Graham Bell approached Western Union to sell the company the patent of his invention, the telephone, its leaders offered him $100,000 but he turned them down. Two years later, realizing their mistake and having greater knowledge of the impact of Bell's invention, they offered him $25 million!

SERENDIPITY **FACTOR**

Coca-Cola was started by accident. About 100 years ago, Coca-Cola was known as a hangover remedy and a hung-over customer asked for Coca-Cola at a soda fountain. In his rush to assist the customer, the soda fountain man added fizzy water rather than keep the customer waiting by going to the water tap at the back. That's how Coke was born.

a

Nokia is Europe's largest company today in terms of market capitalization. Say the name Nokia and most people think of mobile phones, but that's only part of the story. Before Nokia could become the epitome of a dynamic, global telecommunications business, it first had to show a classic example of flexibility.

In the mid-20th century, the conglomerate earned its living by making things like Wellington boots. However, Nokia's leaders realized this wouldn't be a workable model for the future, so they came up with a total change of business model and strategy. Aware of the increasing significance of communications and the potential of digital electronics, the leaders completely transformed the company. In a short time, this flexibility translated into a decisive competitive edge.

b

Years ago, a chemist dropped a flask containing a liquid plastic substance. When he picked up the pieces, he noticed they stuck together. As a result of this accident, he invented shatterproof glass.

A group of 3M researchers was trying to develop a synthetic rubber for jet-aircraft hoses when a beaker containing some of the trial substance fell on a lab technician's tennis shoe. No standard cleaning solvent would remove it. With further refinement, the substance became Scotchgard® fabric protector.

Clarence Crane, a chocolate dealer, sold peppermints during the summer when sales of chocolate declined. He had the mints pressed into shape by a local pill manufacturer.

In 1912, the machine malfunctioned and pressed out peppermint rings instead of solid mints. Instead of complaining about deformed mints, Crane knew he had a unique product, which he called Life Savers.

Bette Nesmith, hoping to save her job as a bank secretary, covered her typos with a mixture of water-based paint and a coloring agent that blended perfectly with the bank's stationery.

It worked so well that she started bottling and selling it out of her garage. Years later, the Gillette company bought Nesmith Paper Coloring for $47.5 million.

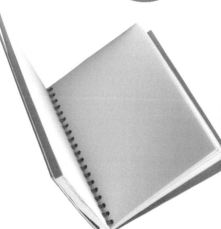

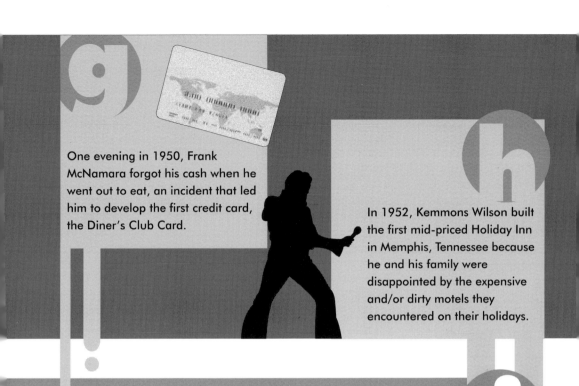

One evening in 1950, Frank McNamara forgot his cash when he went out to eat, an incident that led him to develop the first credit card, the Diner's Club Card.

In 1952, Kemmons Wilson built the first mid-priced Holiday Inn in Memphis, Tennessee because he and his family were disappointed by the expensive and/or dirty motels they encountered on their holidays.

George Thomas was searching for an effective way for people to apply deodorant. He was very frustrated in his search for a solution until he realized he was holding the answer in his hand. George borrowed the concept of the ballpoint pen and created roll-on deodorant.

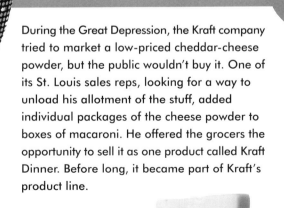

During the Great Depression, the Kraft company tried to market a low-priced cheddar-cheese powder, but the public wouldn't buy it. One of its St. Louis sales reps, looking for a way to unload his allotment of the stuff, added individual packages of the cheese powder to boxes of macaroni. He offered the grocers the opportunity to sell it as one product called Kraft Dinner. Before long, it became part of Kraft's product line.

ALL THE BEST
ON BUILDING
YOUR BRICKS
TO BRIDGES

G.L.O.S.S.A.R.Y.

Balanced Scorecard	Tool for measuring and managing the business
BOHICA	Bend Over Here It Comes Again
Business Blunders	The wrong action, producing the wrong results
Business Case	Rationale for a new strategy
Catch-up Strategy	When an organization constantly lags behind the competition and tries to close the gap but never succeeds
Change Fatigue	An affliction of staff members who have seen it all before and been part of too many implementation initiatives
Communication Strategy	The statement indicating what leaders want the communication for the initiative to achieve
Critical Mass	80 percent of the people in the organization moving in the right direction toward change
CSF	Critical Success Factors
Double Agents	Small group of long-term employees who have "seen it all before" and feel skeptical about the change. But once the organization proves change will happen, they switch to being **Mavericks.**
Dynamics of Change	The distribution of people's reaction to change
Flavor of the Month	Name for a concern that an initiative will last only four weeks
Groupies	The largest group of employees who neither enthusiastically embrace the change nor oppose it

Implementation Compass	A generic tool that provides you with the structure your strategy. It's the tool for making your strategy come alive
Implementation Strategy	The complete detailed action plan that directs and leads the organization in the actions it takes to achieve its anticipated results
Innovation	Breaking the traditional pattern of how things get done
KICC	Keep it confusing and complicated
KISS	Keep it simple stupid
Mavericks	Employees who willingly and enthusiastically support the implementantion and take action
NATO	No Action, Talk Only
Operational Scorecard	Measures at the operational level used to gauge the impact of short-term initiatives
OROTC - (pronounced OR-OT-IC)	A tool for ensuring staff members take the right action
Recent-cy Factor	When being reviewed by your boss, how you've performed in the last three months typically has a greater influence than how you performed during the rest of the year
Recogniton	Non-financial kudos
Reward	Financial kudos
Saboteurs	Employees who are out to derail the change and want to keep the status quo

Serendipity Factor	An accident with a pleasing result
Six Sigma	A structured approach to improving business performance, driven by measurement and process improvement
SSDD	Same Shit Different Day
Strategic Implentation Review (SIR)	A structured two-hour meeting conducted regularly by leaders to track the strategy implementation
T&T	Tools and techniques required to implement the change
This works!	Suggestions to assist the implementation
TINA	There Is No Alternative
Voice of the Customer	An expression used to describe the customer's views
Watch Out!	Areas to avoid
WEX-FM	What's Expected From Me
WII-FM	What's In It For Me

Summary

Chapter 1

Bricks to Bridges starts by clearly demonstrating a need to transform strategy implementation as it is today into viable results. It asks these tough questions:

· Why does implementation have a high failure rate?
· Why do organizations repeat the same mistakes?
· Why do leaders tolerate a 90% failure rate?

Yet all is not lost. The author's Implementation Compass can save the day for leaders willing to use this tool well. This chapter persuades them that they can reverse that 90% failure rate; the chapters that follow specifically tell them how.

Chapter 2

How the implementation process actually works has shifted. Exactly what has changed? The fundamentals themselves.

Extensive research conducted between 2001 and 2004 gives leaders three important research findings: They need to gain support within the organization for implementation, they need to communicate changes well, and they need to overcome resistance from staff.

Traditionally, employees simply didn't know what they were supposed to do to put a new strategy into action. By leaving behind the eight traditional fundamentals and following the six new fundamentals, leaders can bring strategy to life through the people who do the work—the staff.

Chapter 3

Focused on the first new fundamental—taking the right action to achieve the right results—this chapter answers these questions:

· What results define success for the implementation?
· How will we know we are achieving the right results?
· What actions need to be taken to achieve these results?

It introduces the shortcut concept of OROTC—Objective, Result, Owner, Timeline, Categorization—as a formula and guide for leaders when implementing strategy. The examples throughout this chapter make the theories tangible for every leader.

Chapter 4

In addressing the second fundamental—the human factor in strategy implementation—the author spells out:

· Why people resist change
· How they respond to change in general
· How specific groups of people respond to change

Within organizations, these specific groups include:

· Saboteurs
· Mavericks
· Double Agents
· Groupies

How do leaders effectively lead each of these differing groups? Valuable answers to that question form the meat of this chapter.

Chapter 5

The biz case for a new strategy implementation explains why an organization's leaders have decided to cross a new bridge and adjust the way they do business. Specifically, the biz case presents reasons that help prepare employees to make concrete changes that will advance the implementation process.

Throughout this chapter, leaders are instructed to follow these well-explained steps:

· Identify the business case
· Identify what's in it for me (WII-FM)
· Tell staff members what's expected from them (WEX-FM)
· Provide the tools and techniques needed to succeed

This chapter also features case studies of several successful implementations conducted in organizations.

Chapter 6

What's the point of implementing a new strategy if those assigned to implement it don't even know what it is? This chapter conveys how to set in motion a strategic communication plan and process that's coordinated, structured and consistent.

The author spells out what modes simply don't work, then recommends an effective method called the cascade kit. He explains how to make this kit—and others modes—highly effective.

Tapping into the extensive list of creative ideas featured in this chapter makes the leaders' communication job easier. The goal: Keeping communications alive so staff members know what to do.

Chapter 7

Focused on measurement, this chapter shows ways to measure the performance of a business and its implementation beyond pure financial performance. It explains how to effectively use the Balanced Scorecard and related operational scorecards.

These scorecards assist organizational leaders in selecting the right measures to put in action and achieve their implementation goals. Case studies feature Xerox, FedEx, a call center, a fast food chain and a manufacturer.

Chapter 8

How do leaders align an organization's culture with the changes required in relation to changes in its product life cycles—especially as products change faster and faster in the marketplace? This chapter addresses the culture life cycle that must change if a strategy implementation is to succeed. Strong indicators of the culture's life cycle are the inflection point and the point of convergence.

The author explains how to study these indicators to show when changes have to be initiated. A key message is to make sure leaders manage the activities as they overlap between the "new" and the "old" ways of doing things. This requires instituting the both/and approach so important pieces don't fall through the cracks.

Chapter 9

Focusing on the behavioral aspects of changing an organization's structure, this chapter discusses changing people's attitudes, values and behaviors as well as changing the environment (and a combination of both approaches).

The author suggests following this four-step process aimed at affecting employees' behaviors:

1. Identify current values
2. Influence attitudes through awareness and knowledge, leading to rational thought that supports change and encouragement from peers
3. Reinforce right behaviors through measurements, plus recognition and rewards
4. Use Values Inculcation Model to provide ongoing attention to performance in the changing culture

Ways to "change the environment" and do a combination of behavioral and environmental approaches are presented through several case studies.

Chapter 10

Continuing to align processes in your organization is critical as the strategy implementation moves forward. One method that helps do that is Six Sigma—a structural approach to improving business performance driven by measurements and process improvements.

The author recommends taking the best practices from Six Sigma without necessarily adopting the method itself. Each of the following practices is explained in the chapter:

1. Link to the P&L
2. Structured process for improvement
3. Measurement system and use of absolute numbers
4. Quantum versus incremental process changes
5. Combination of hard and soft sides
6. Emphasis on the customer—end to end
7. Supporting infrastructure

Chapter 11

Organizations perform at different levels of competency. The author defines these levels as Standard, Best Of Class, Best In The World and Out Of This World. At the other end of the spectrum, he assigns poor performances the lowest level—"Criminal"!

How does a company improve its performance and catch up to others performing at the next highest level? Through streamlining its processes (which is easier said than done). Some high-achieving organizations go beyond benchmarking that will mostly only make them "Best In Class" and leapfrog to the next level, using innovation to make them "Best In The World."

All this classification starts with benchmarking existing processes, then evaluating benchmarked results against other companies. The 12 steps of benchmarking in this chapter spell out how your organization can set up benchmarking.

What characteristics do Best In The World organizations have in common? They are:

1. Global Recognition
2. Excellence in One Key Area Only
3. Full Systems and Structure Support
4. High Value Creation
5. High Ethics
6. Strong People and High Morals
7. Social Responsibility

Examples are also provided from a number of Best In The World companies.

Chapter 12

Setting up an effective way to recognize and reward staff members reinforces the entire implementation process from start to finish—when it's executed well., When it's done poorly, however, lack of proper recognition can sabotage your results significantly.

This comprehensive chapter details the do's and don'ts of how to appropriately reinforce the behavior of your employees so your organization can succeed. Putting the ideas it presents into practice makes every leader and manager's job easier.

Chapter 13

A Strategic Implementation Review (SIR) helps an organization's leaders ensure that the change they want to implement is heading in the right direction. An SIR takes the form of a regular structured two-hour meeting to discuss changing conditions and to make adjustments to the strategy. The meetings' discussions revolve around the SIR principles, objectives and components that are carefully explained in this chapter.

The author affirms that conducting SIRs as a regular business practice simply means the difference between success and failure.

Chapter 14

Who would admit to being involved in an implementation failure? Before you answer "no one," consider the Serendipity Factor—results of accidental discoveries that ended in making millions of dollars for a company. On the other side of the coin, a number of Business Blunders unearthed by the author show the consequences of an organization taking wrong turns and losing a golden opportunity.

This light-hearted chapter filled with recognizable examples will launch you on the road to building your own strategy implementation—from bricks to bridges.

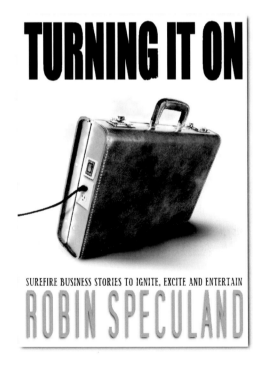

Build your Communication

with a set of words of wisdom posters

"The **ultimate competitive advantage** lies in an organization's ability to **learn** and to **rapidly transform** that learning into **action**."

"A **single conversation** across the table with a **wise man** is worth **a month's study of books**"

Life is change. Growth is optional. **Choose wisely.**

"It is not the **strongest species** that survive, nor the **most intelligent**, but the ones **most responsive** to change."

Implementation without

Vision	= Confusion
Skills	= Anxiety
Resources	= Frustration
Motivation	= Slow Change
Leadership	= Flavour of the month
Action	= False Starts

"To **change** and **change for the better** are two different things"

"Everything in life is **mind over matter**. If you **don't mind**, it **doesn't matter**."

"Be the **change** you are **trying to create**"

"If you **always do** what you have always done, then you will always get **what you always got**"

"Companies fail to **successfully implement** strategy not because of bad strategy, but bad execution"

"**Speak** and they will **question**. Do and they **will follow**."

"After all is **said and done**, more is said than done"

Implementation Cards
comes in a pack of fifty-two cards.

1 — Lack of teamwork among departments

2 — Do not know enough about our customers' expectations

3 — Lack of support from managers

4 — Staff are afraid to change

5 — Lack of inspiration & motivation from senior management

6 — Lack of vision

7 — Lack of recognition for suggestions

8 — No recognition from my boss

To order, visit www.bridgesconsultancy.com

For enquiries, e-mail us at bridges@bridgesconsultancy.com

Index